COMPUTERS IN CONTEXT

Carl A. Sharpf

Gary Ewen
Colorado Christian University

ADDISON-WESLEY

An imprint of Addison Wesley Longman, Inc.

Reading, Massachusetts • Menlo Park, California • New York • Harlow, England
Don Mills, Ontario • Sydney • Mexico City • Madrid • Amsterdam

Acquisition Editor: Anita Devine
Marketing Manager: Michelle Hudson
Production Supervision/Copyediting: Diane Freed
Indexer: Irv Hershman
Composition: Michael Strong
Cover Design: Gina Hagen
Manufacturing Supervisor: Sheila Spinney

Products mentioned in *Computers in Context*

America Online is a registered service mark of America Online, Inc.
AST is a registered trademark of AST Research, Inc.
AutoCAD is a registered trademark of Autodesk, Inc.
Claris, Claris Works, and FileMaker Pro are registered trademarks of Claris Corporation.
Compaq is a registered trademark of the Compaq Computer Corporation.
CompuServe is a registered trademark of CompuServe, Inc.
Hewlett-Packard is a registered trademark of the Hewlett-Packard Company.
IBM and OS/2 are registered trademarks and ThinkPad and PowerPC are trademarks of International Business Machines Corporation.
Intel, the Intel Inside logo, Intel 486, Pentium and Pentium II are registered trademarks of Intel Corporation.
Kodak Photo CD is a registered trademark of Kodak.
Lotus, 1-2-3, cc:mail, and SmartSuite are registered trademarks of Lotus Development Corporation.
Macintosh, Mac, Apple, the Apple logo, PowerBook, and Power Macintosh are registered trademarks of Apple Computer, Inc.
Microsoft, MS-DOS, Windows, Windows 95, Microsoft PowerPoint, Microsoft Word, Microsoft Excel, and Microsoft Access are registered trademarks of Microsoft Corporation.
Novell and Personal Netware are trademarks of Novell, Inc.
ScanMan is a registered trademark of Logitech.
UNIX is a registered trademark of UNIX Systems Laboratories.
Win Book is a registered trademark of MicroElectronics, Inc.
Xerox is a registered trademark of Xerox Corporation.

All other brand, company or product names are trademarks or registered trademarks of their respective companies.

ISBN 0-201-34584-6

Addison-Wesley Publishing Company
One Jacob Way
Reading, MA 01867
http://hepg.awl.com/select
is@awl.com

1 2 3 4 5 6 7 8 9 10-DOW-01009998

Preface to the Instructor

Computers in Context

Change is not what is used to be. As we begin the new millenium, powerful forces—enabled by new technologies—are changing the way we work, play, and live. These technologies are evolving and growing at an incredible rate. Indeed, some say that the only constant is change.

The digital technology of computers is embedded in everything from handheld portable telephone/pagers to TVs and stereos, from refrigerators to washers and dryers. Our entertainment is rapidly becoming digitized, as are our traditional information sources such as magazines and newspapers. The world's economy is being radically changed by this digital convergence. If individuals can understand and synthesize these changes and the role of technology in the new digital economy, success can follow. That understanding must start somewhere.

Students don't normally take a computer course merely to read about computers. They are usually anxious to get their hands on the machines, turn them on, and begin using them. Experience has shown, however, that the best learning starts with a foundation of knowledge that offers the student a context within which further learning can be pursued. Too often, people make the mistake of skipping that crucial first step of establishing a firm foundation of knowledge. This is unfortunate, because the pace of technological change is rapid and without a foundational knowledge base it is very difficult to build further knowledge and skills when the tectonic shifts in technology occur. The purpose of *Computers in Context* is to provide learners with that crucial foundation of knowledge.

Computers in Context is designed to assist people in making the first steps to understanding the myriad technologies and change elements that converge to make the new digital economy a reality. *Computers in Context* is designed for the beginner who may be somewhat intimidated by all of the new technologies. It is also designed for the person who already has some computer competencies but has gaps in his or her foundational knowledge of computer technologies. The ideas and concepts presented in this book are written in easy-to-read plain language with the goal of dispelling much of the mystery that surrounds computers. It is meant to be the first step in a rewarding journey toward becoming literate and competent in the new technologies.

Computers in Context is a starting point for all learners to help reinforce their foundational knowledge of computers in combination with their hands-on lab sessions. *Computers in Context* can be used as a stand-alone concepts text or can be packaged with any combination of the *SELECT Lab Series* published by Addison Wesley Longman. The *SELECT Lab Series* includes specifically designed hands-on books covering a variety of computer applications.

The Select Lab Series

The *SELECT Lab Series* is an applications series designed specifically to make learning easy and enjoyable, a natural outcome of thoughtful, meaningful activity. The goal for the series is to create a learning environment in which students can explore the essentials of software applications, use critical thinking, and gain confidence and proficiency.

Greater access to ideas and information is changing the way people work. With today's business and communication application software, you have greater integration capabilities and easier access to Internet resources than ever before. The *SELECT Lab Series* helps you take advantage of these valuable resources, with special assignments devoted to the Internet and with additional connectivity resources that can be accessed through our Web site, **http://hepg.awl.com/select/.**

The *SELECT Lab Series* offers dozens of proven and class-tested materials, from the latest operating systems and browsers, to the most popular applications software for word processing, spreadsheets, databases, presentation graphics, desktop publishing, and integrated packages, to HTML, to programming. For your lab course, you can choose what you want to combine; your choice of lab matnuals will be sent to the bookstore, combined in a TechSuite, allowing students to purchase all books in one convenient package at a discount.

The most popular *SELECT Lab Series* titles are available in three levels of coverage. The *SELECT Brief features* 4 projects that quickly lay the foundation of an application in 3 to 5 contact hours. The *standard edition SELECT* expands on material covered in the brief edition with 5 to 8 projects that teach intermediate skills in just 6 to 9 contact hours. *SELECT Plus* provides 10 to 12 projects that cover intermediate to advanced material in 12 to 14 contact hours.

Your Addison Wesley Longman representative will be happy to work with you and your bookstore manager to provide the most current menu of *SELECT Lab Series* offerings, outline the ordering process, and provide pricing, ISBNs, and delivery information. Or call 1-800-447-2226 or visit our Web site at http://www.awl.com/.

Organization

The "Overview of Windows 95," which appears in some *SELECT Lab Series* modules, familiarizes students with Windows 95 before launching into the application. Students learn the basics of starting Windows 95, using a mouse, using the essential features of Windows 95, getting help, and exiting Windows 95.

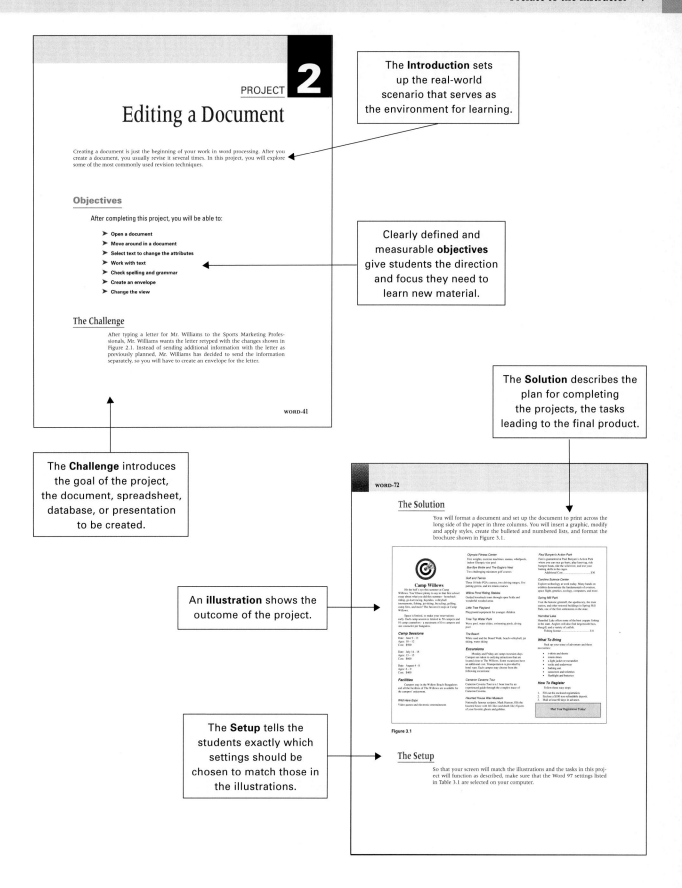

PROJECT **2**

Editing a Document

Creating a document is just the beginning of your work in word processing. After you create a document, you usually revise it several times. In this project, you will explore some of the most commonly used revision techniques.

Objectives

After completing this project, you will be able to:

➤ Open a document
➤ Move around in a document
➤ Select text to change the attributes
➤ Work with text
➤ Check spelling and grammar
➤ Create an envelope
➤ Change the view

The Challenge

After typing a letter for Mr. Williams to the Sports Marketing Professionals, Mr. Williams wants the letter retyped with the changes shown in Figure 2.1. Instead of sending additional information with the letter as previously planned, Mr. Williams has decided to send the information separately, so you will have to create an envelope for the letter.

WORD-41

The **Introduction** sets up the real-world scenario that serves as the environment for learning.

Clearly defined and measurable **objectives** give students the direction and focus they need to learn new material.

The **Challenge** introduces the goal of the project, the document, spreadsheet, database, or presentation to be created.

The **Solution** describes the plan for completing the projects, the tasks leading to the final product.

WORD-72

The Solution

You will format a document and set up the document to print across the long side of the paper in three columns. You will insert a graphic, modify and apply styles, create the bulleted and numbered lists, and format the brochure shown in Figure 3.1.

Figure 3.1

An **illustration** shows the outcome of the project.

The Setup

So that your screen will match the illustrations and the tasks in this project will function as described, make sure that the Word 97 settings listed in Table 3.1 are selected on your computer.

The **Setup** tells the students exactly which settings should be chosen to match those in the illustrations.

vi

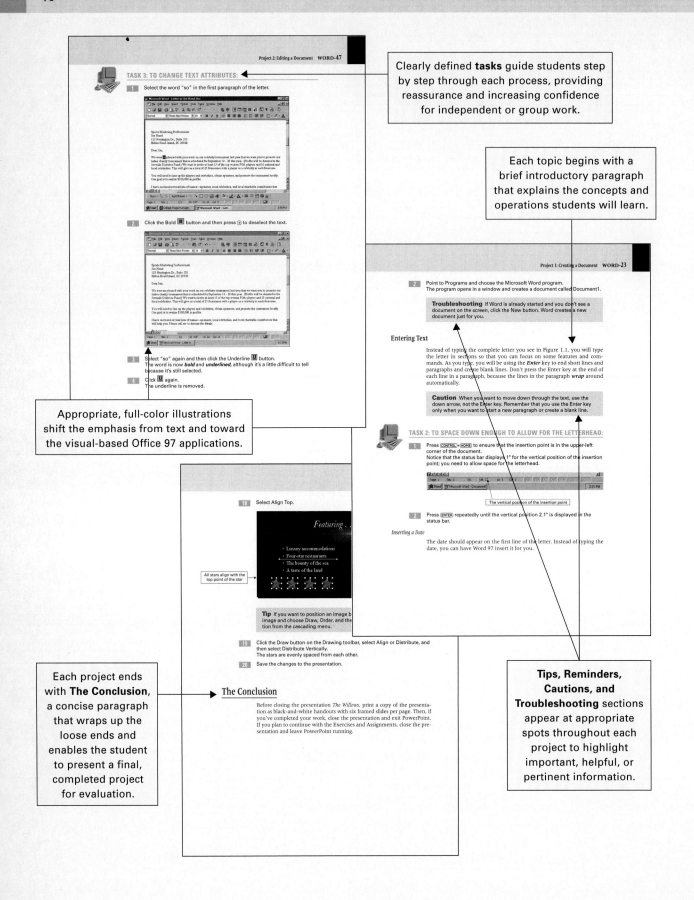

Clearly defined **tasks** guide students step by step through each process, providing reassurance and increasing confidence for independent or group work.

Each topic begins with a brief introductory paragraph that explains the concepts and operations students will learn.

Appropriate, full-color illustrations shift the emphasis from text and toward the visual-based Office 97 applications.

Tips, Reminders, Cautions, and Troubleshooting sections appear at appropriate spots throughout each project to highlight important, helpful, or pertinent information.

Each project ends with **The Conclusion**, a concise paragraph that wraps up the loose ends and enables the student to present a final, completed project for evaluation.

A bulleted **summary list** further reinforces the objectives and the material presented in the project.

Key Terms are boldface and italicized throughout each project and then listed for handy review in the summary section at the end of the project.

Twenty-four **study questions** (Multiple Choice, Short Answer, and For Discussion) bring the content of the project into focus again and allow for independent or group review of the material learned.

Review Exercises present hands-on tasks for building on the skills acquired in the project.

Assignments invoke critical thinking and encourage integration of project skills.

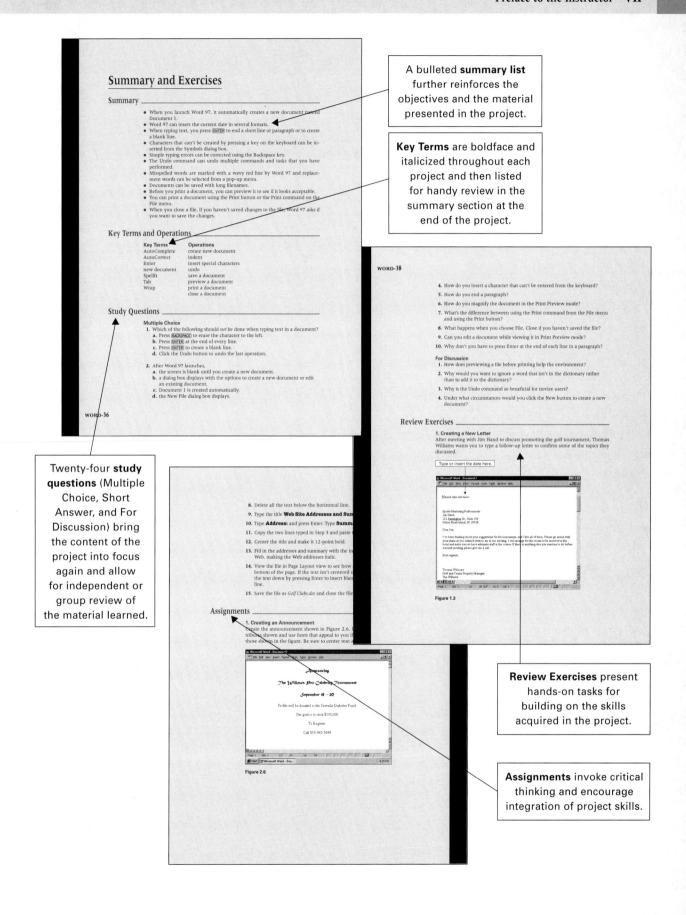

Summary and Exercises

Summary

- When you launch Word 97, it automatically creates a new document named Document 1.
- Word 97 can insert the current date in several formats.
- When typing text, you press (ENTER) to end a short line or paragraph or to create a blank line.
- Characters that can't be created by pressing a key on the keyboard can be inserted from the Symbols dialog box.
- Simple typing errors can be corrected using the Backspace key.
- The Undo command can undo multiple commands and tasks that you have performed.
- Misspelled words are marked with a wavy red line by Word 97 and replacement words can be selected from a pop-up menu.
- Documents can be saved with long filenames.
- Before you print a document, you can preview it to see if it looks acceptable.
- You can print a document using the Print button or the Print command on the File menu.
- When you close a file, if you haven't saved changes to the file, Word 97 asks if you want to save the changes.

Key Terms and Operations

Key Terms	Operations
AutoComplete	create new document
AutoCorrect	indent
Enter	insert special characters
new document	undo
SpellIt	save a document
Tab	preview a document
Wrap	print a document
	close a document

Study Questions

Multiple Choice

1. Which of the following should *not* be done when typing text in a document?
   a. Press (BACKSPACE) to erase the character to the left.
   b. Press (ENTER) at the end of every line.
   c. Press (ENTER) to create a blank line.
   d. Click the Undo button to undo the last operation.

2. After Word 97 launches,
   a. the screen is blank until you create a new document.
   b. a dialog box displays with the options to create a new document or edit an existing document.
   c. Document 1 is created automatically.
   d. the New File dialog box displays.

WORD-36

WORD-38

4. How do you insert a character that can't be entered from the keyboard?

5. How do you end a paragraph?

6. How do you magnify the document in the Print Preview mode?

7. What's the difference between using the Print command from the File menu and using the Print button?

8. What happens when you choose File, Close if you haven't saved the file?

9. Can you edit a document while viewing it in Print Preview mode?

10. Why don't you have to press Enter at the end of each line in a paragraph?

For Discussion

1. How does previewing a file before printing help the environment?

2. Why would you want to ignore a word that isn't in the dictionary rather than to add it to the dictionary?

3. Why is the Undo command so beneficial to novice users?

4. Under what circumstances would you click the New button to create a new document?

Review Exercises

1. Creating a New Letter

After meeting with Jim Hand to discuss promoting the golf tournament, Thomas Williams wants you to type a follow-up letter to confirm some of the topics they discussed.

Figure 1.3

---

8. Delete all the text below the horizontal line.

9. Type the title **Web Site Addresses and Sum**

10. Type **Address:** and press Enter. Type **Summ**

11. Copy the two lines typed in Step 3 and paste

12. Center the title and make it 12-point bold.

13. Fill in the addresses and summary with the in Web, making the Web addresses italic.

14. View the file in Page Layout view to see how bottom of the page. If the text isn't centered the text down by pressing Enter to insert blan line.

15. Save the file as *Golf Clubs.doc* and close the file

Assignments

1. Creating an Announcement

Create the announcement shown in Figure 2.6. tributes shown and use fonts that appeal to you if those shown in the figure. Be sure to center text

Figure 2.6

Organization

Each application is then covered in depth in a number of projects that teach beginning to intermediate skills. An overview introduces the basic concepts of the application and provides hands-on instructions to put students to work using the application immediately. Students learn problem-solving techniques while working through projects that provide practical, real-life scenarios that they can relate to.

Web assignments appear throughout the text at the end of each project, giving students practice using the Internet.

Approach

The *SELECT Lab Series* uses a document-centered approach to learning. Each project begins with a list of measurable objectives, a realistic scenario called the Challenge, a well-defined plan called the Solution, and an illustration of the final product. The Setup enables students to verify that the settings on the computer match those needed for the project. Each project is arranged in carefully divided, highly visual objective-based tasks that foster confidence and self-reliance. Each project closes with a wrap-up of the project called the Conclusion, followed by summary questions, exercises, and assignments geared to reinforcing the information taught through the project.

Other Features

In addition to the document-centered, visual approach of each project, this book contains the following features:

- An overview of the application so that students feel comfortable and confident as they function in the working environment.
- Keycaps and toolbar button icons within each step so that the student can quickly perform the required action.
- A comprehensive and well-organized end-of-the-project Summary and Exercises section for reviewing, integrating, and applying new skills.
- An illustration or description of the results of each step so that students know they're on the right track all the time.

Supplements

You get extra support for this text from supplemental materials, including the *Instructor's Manual* and the Instructor's Data Disk.

The *Instructor's Manual* includes a Test Bank for each project in the student text, Expanded Student Objectives, Answers to Study Questions, and Additional Assessment Techniques. The Test Bank contains two separate tests with answers and consists of multiple-choice, true/false, and fill-in questions referenced to pages in the student text. Transparency Masters illustrate key concepts and screen captures from the text.

The Instructor's Data Disk contains student data files, completed data files for Review Exercises and assignments, and the test files from the *Instructor's Manual* in ASCII format.

For Internet and browser-related lab manuals, see the SELECT Web site for supplementary materials.

Acknowledgments

Addison-Wesley Publishing Company would like to thank the following reviewers for their valuable contributions to the *SELECT Lab Series*.

James Agnew
Northern Virginia
Community College

Joseph Aieta
Babson College

Dr. Muzaffar Ali
Bellarmine College

Tom Ashby
Oklahoma CC

Bob Barber
Lane CC

Robert Caruso
Santa Rosa Junior College

Robert Chi
California State
Long Beach

Jill Davis
State University of New York
at Stony Brook

Fredia Dillard
Samford University

Peter Drexel
Plymouth State College

David Egle
University of Texas, Pan
American

Linda Ericksen
Lane Community College

Jonathan Frank
Suffolk University

Patrick Gilbert
University of Hawaii

Maureen Greenbaum
Union County College

Sally Ann Hanson
Mercer County CC

Sunil Hazari
East Carolina University

Gloria Henderson
Victor Valley College

Bruce Herniter
University of Hartford

Rick Homkes
Purdue University

Lisa Jackson
Henderson CC

Martha Johnson
(technical reviewer)
Delta State University

Cynthia Kachik
Santa Fe CC

Bill Knoepfer
College of Notre Dame

Charles Lake
Faulkner State Junior
College

Ron Leake
Johnson County CC

Randy Marak
Hill College

Bennett Kramer
Massasoit CC

Jim McCullough
Porter and Chester
Institute

Gail Miles
Lenoir-Rhyne College

Steve Moore
University of South
Florida

Michael Martel
University of Southern Maine

Gloria Oman
Portland State University

Bettye Parham
Daytona Beach
Community College

Leonard Presby
William Paterson College

Charles Mattox, Jr.
St. Mary's University

Michael Reilly
University of Denver

John Passafiume
Clemson University

Dennis Santomauro
Kean College of
New Jersey

Anthony Nowakowski
Buffalo State College

Gary Schubert
Alderson-Broaddus
College

Dick Ricketts
Lane CC

Cynthia Thompson
Carl Sandburg College

Louis Pryor
Garland County CC

JoAnn Weatherwax
Saddleback College

T. Michael Smith
Austin CC

James Wood
Tri-County Technical
College

Pamela Schmidt
Oakton CC

Allen Zilbert
Long Island University

David Whitney
San Francisco State
University

Marion Tucker
Northern Oklahoma College

Dedicated to:

My mother for teaching me to love to read

My father for teaching me to work hard

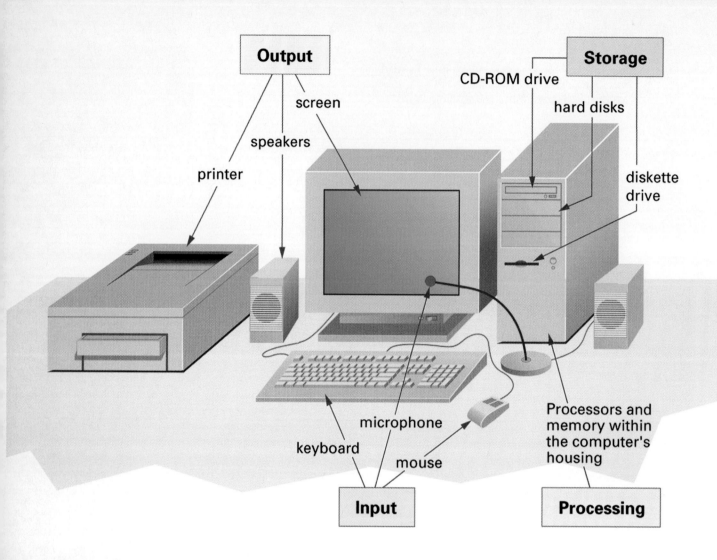

Main System

Multimedia

Network

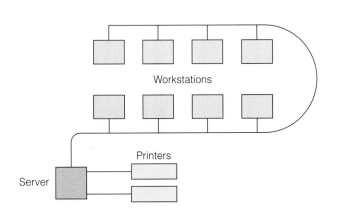

Workstations

Printers

Server

URL:

`http://www.intel.com/homecomputing/index.htm`

Protocol   ISP address (domain)   Path, directory, file name

The Internet

Contents

Computers in Context

Objectives

After completing this section, you will be able to

➤ **Define hardware and software**

➤ **Understand how the four major hardware components work together**

➤ **Define operating systems, application software packages, and programming languages**

➤ **Recognize different types of computers according to their size**

➤ **Understand multimedia, networking, and telecommunications**

➤ **Understand the basic concepts of the Internet**

➤ **Understand where technology is "going" in the next few years**

➤ **Understand that technology has many benefits and many risks**

Computers can be intimidating and confusing to many people. In fact, many people suffer from a malady known as cyberphobia. *Cyberphobia* is the illogical and usually inexplicable fear of computers, and primarily afflicts people who do not understand some of the basic concepts of computers.

Computers don't have to be intimidating at all. Actually, computers are quite stupid. They aren't worthy of awe or fear—people just need to understand a few things about them in order to demystify them. A computer can seem very mysterious because so much power is wrapped up into such a small package. The first time you use a computer, you may feel a little apprehensive. You may not even want to touch the computer for fear of pressing the wrong key and breaking something. Fortunately, computers are relatively sturdy and their basic parts are fairly easy to understand. Before long, using a computer will become as comfortable for you as driving a car.

Overview

There are four major classifications of computers: supercomputers, mainframe computers, minicomputers, and microcomputers.

Supercomputers are very large and very powerful (see Figure 1). Supercomputers usually require very high-tech environmental control. In fact, many supercomputers require liquid nitrogen to keep them cool enough to operate. Supercomputers are very expensive, and usually only the largest commercial enterprises or scientific and engineering environments can afford them. They are the most powerful computers in the world and usually are used in huge multi-user environments to do sophisticated calculations such as those needed in massive engineering simulations and scientific experiments. Supercomputers cost millions of dollars.

Figure 1 This Cray supercomputer may not look impressive, but it can calculate more than a trillion calculations per second.

Mainframe computers (see Figure 2) are used in large commercial organizations for significant data processing needs. They are fairly expensive and usually require air-conditioned and climate-controlled computer rooms to house their large systems. Mainframe computers usually cost hundreds of thousands of dollars.

Until a few years ago, *minicomputers* were popular. Smaller (about the size of a file cabinet) and less expensive than mainframes, minicomputers usually require no special environmental control other than a normal office environment. Minicomputers may be used in a variety of multi-user commercial environments for day-to-day data processing needs. For the most part, minicomputers have lost ground to the less expensive and increasingly powerful microcomputers available today.

Microcomputers are usually small and require no special environmental control. They are relatively

inexpensive and yet very powerful in meeting the everyday needs of most people. As illustrated in Figure 3, microcomputers come in a variety of sizes and are used in a wide variety of ways by people of all ages. Microcomputers have emerged as the fastest growing segment of the computer industry. Also known as *personal computers,* microcomputers are typically used by one person at a time and range in size from small handheld units to larger, more powerful tower units that stand upright on the floor. Microcomputers range in price from a few hundred dollars to a few thousand dollars.

Regardless of their classification (or how expensive they might be), all computers function by the same basic principles:

The first of these principles is that a *computer* is a programmable, electronic device that is capable of storing, retrieving, and processing data. The ability to program a computer means that the computer can be instructed (by a human) to perform a variety of tasks. A computer program is a sequenced set of instructions that controls the computer. The computer *program* instructs the computer and tells it what to do, when to do it, and how to do it. Computer programs are usually referred to as software.

The second fundamental principle of computers is that software and hardware work together to make the computer function. Computer equipment such as the display screen or monitor, the keyboard, the printer, and other physical parts is called *hardware*. Hardware is the tangible equipment that makes up the computer system. *Software* is the sequenced sets of instructions (programs) that govern the operation of the computer.

Figure 2 A mainframe computer.

Figure 3 The Toshiba Libretto, one of the smallest full-function sub-notebook computers. The Libretto is very portable and can even fit in a suit pocket.

The third basic principle of computers is that all computers are designed to process data. Each data element by itself is relatively meaningless. Not until the data elements are combined do they begin to take on meaning. **Data** are the raw facts, figures, or characters that are processed by the computer into (hopefully) useful information. **Information** is processed data that has meaning or conveys knowledge.

The fourth basic principle of computers is that all computers are actually systems of components that work together to serve you and meet many of your needs. A **system** is a regularly interacting or interrelated group of parts that form a unified whole. In other words, computers are a group of different parts (subcomponents) that work together toward a common purpose. That common purpose is to transform data into useful information.

Computer systems transform data into useful information through a system flow called the **IPOS cycle**. IPOS stands for *input, processing, output, and storage*. That is, you have to get data into the computer (*input*) in order to process it into useful information. The IPOS Cycle and IPOS hardware is represented by Figure 4.

Traditionally, computers have been described as having four main hardware components: **input, processing, output**, and **secondary storage**. Figure 5 shows the IPOS cycle from the view of the personal computer system.

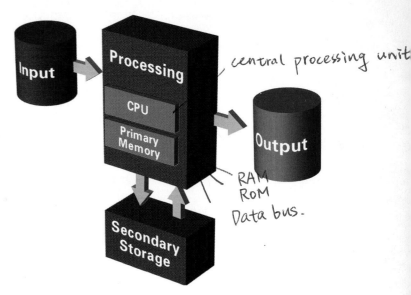

Figure 4 The IPOS cycle.

Because **data communications** among computers is becoming so prevalent, we also consider communications hardware as a primary component in the computer system. Because data communications hardware performs both input and output operations in the computer system, it should be considered a special (fifth) category of computer hardware.

Once the computer processes the data into useful information it must output the information in a form that is useful for humans to use. Anything used to get data into a computer system is called an

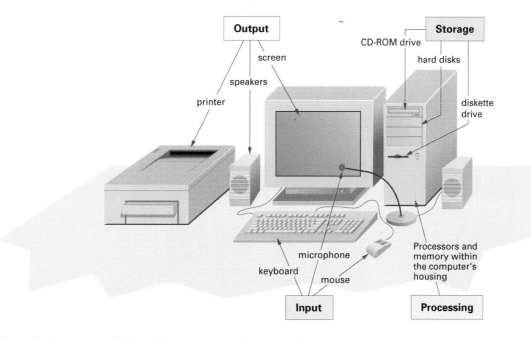

Figure 5 The IPOS cycle from the perspective of a personal computer system.

input device. Anything used to transform data into useful information is called a *processing device*. Anything used to get the processed information out to the human is called an *output device*.

 FYI You might compare this IPOS cycle to one of today's popular bread makers. You put the raw ingredients into the bread maker (input), and then you turn on the device. The bread maker processes the raw ingredients by mixing them into dough and then baking the dough. Through this process the bread maker produces a useful loaf of freshly baked bread (output).

However, if you put the wrong ingredients in the bread maker to begin with, there is no way the bread maker is going to create a quality loaf of bread. In other words, if you put garbage into the bread maker, the bread maker will only produce processed garbage.

This concept of garbage-in → garbage-out is important. You must be very careful to get the right data into the computer if you want the right information out of the computer.

Hardware

It is easier to understand computer hardware if we sort it into general categories according to function: input hardware, processing hardware (including the central processing unit), memory, output hardware, storage hardware, and communications hardware.

Input Hardware

Various devices are used to input data for processing by the computer. The general trend is toward equipment that is easy to use, fast, and accurate.

Keyboard   The most common way to enter data is with a *keyboard*. As you type, your keystrokes are interpreted (processed) by the computer and corresponding data is displayed on the screen. A computer keyboard is similar to a typewriter keyboard but includes extra keys, such as function keys, cursor control keys, and a numeric (ten-key) keypad for performing computer-related tasks. Figure 6 shows an example of an ergonomically designed keyboard.

Pointing Devices   Most computer software packages display objects on the screen that you can point to with a hand-operated pointing device. Figure 7 shows someone using a *mouse*, which is an input device with a ball on its underside that, when rolled across a surface, detects movement. As the mouse

Natural® Keyboard

Figure 6 An ergonomically designed keyboard.

Figure 7 Movement of the mouse on a flat surface causes corresponding movement of a pointer on the display screen.

moves, a pointer on the display screen moves in a corresponding direction. Today's mouse usually has two buttons. Usually the primary mouse button that performs most tasks is on the left side of the mouse, but increasingly new computer programs use the right mouse button to perform a variety of additional tasks. "Clicking" involves pressing and releasing a mouse button while holding the mouse stationary over a graphic symbol on the display screen. Double-clicking is the process of pressing and releasing the mouse button twice in rapid succession. A mouse is typically used to choose commands or select text. You can also use the mouse to draw pictures if you have drawing software.

A *trackball* has the same function as a mouse, but instead of moving the trackball on a flat surface, you roll a small ball that protrudes from the top of the trackball base. Trackballs are often found on or adjacent to portable computer keyboards, because portable computer users often don't have enough physical space to effectively use a mouse. See Figure 8.

A *trackpad* performs the same functions as a mouse or trackball but the look and feel of a trackpad is quite different. The trackpad looks like a small rectangular plastic membrane, as shown in Figure 9

Figure 8 Trackballs are pointing devices used frequently in portable computers and in many video game machines.

Figure 9 Using your finger on this pad moves the pointer on the display screen. The tabs at the bottom serve the same functions as the mouse buttons.

over which you designate pointer movement (on the screen) by merely touching your finger to the surface of the trackpad and then dragging your finger in the desired direction. Clicking and double-clicking can be performed by simply tapping your finger on the trackpad membrane or by clicking one of the buttons beside the trackpad.

Pen-based computers accept input from a stylus applied directly to a flat panel screen. You can use a stylus to enter handwritten text, draw diagrams, or point to objects on the screen. Figure 10 shows a *personal digital assistant (PDA)*. PDAs are an emerging category of pen-based computers that serve as handheld notebooks, appointment calendars, drawing pads, and sometimes even fax machines and cellular phones.

尖筆

The PDA's pointing device, called a *stylus*, does not have a ballpoint or felt tip like writing pens. It simply has a small, dull point that applies pressure to the screen. Styluses are good input devices in situations where keyboards or a mouse are impractical.

Optical scanners enable the computer to "see" digitally. Light is reflected off drawings, pictures, or text and then captured using light-sensitive electronic devices. The captured image or text is then placed in memory and displayed on the screen. Scanners come in three styles: handheld, which scans as the scanner is manually passed over the image; flatbed, which scans an entire page in one pass; and sheetfed, which scans multiple pages of images or text. Brochures, flyers, or pamphlets often have a greater impact with scanned images. Figure 11 shows all three types of scanners.

Once an image has been scanned into the computer it can be stored and used again. The image can be resized, recolored, and digitally transformed in amazing ways. Figure 11a shows how paper can be fed into the motorized rollers of a sheetfed scanner, which has the added advantage of fitting nicely between the keyboard and the monitor. Figure 11b shows how handheld scanners are manually passed over the image or text to be scanned. With a flatbed scanner, as shown in Figure 11c, the image or text to be scanned is laid face down on the scanner, which looks similar to a small personal copy machine.

When you scan information, the computer does not know whether the input is a picture, text, or something else. If you plan to use scanned text, you will need special *optical character recognition (OCR)*

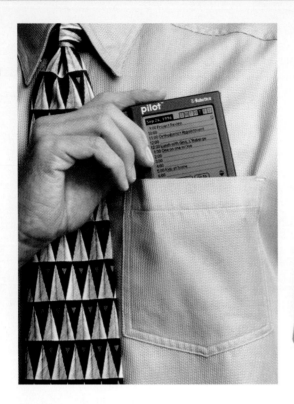

Figure 10 The popular Palm Pilot, made by 3COM/U.S. Robotics, weighs just five ounces and fits in a shirt pocket. This handheld PDA keeps track of a calendar, address book, and an electronic notepad. The Palm Pilot can exchange data with a personal computer with the press of a button.

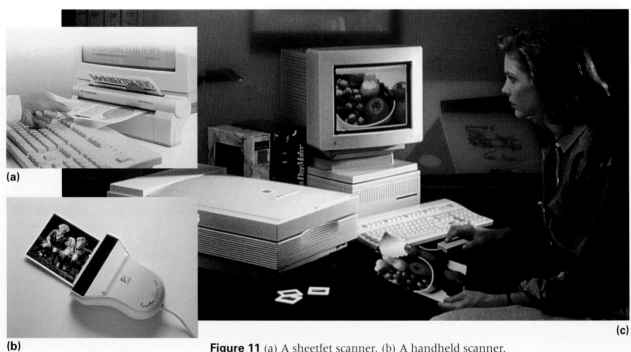

(a)

(b)

(c)

Figure 11 (a) A sheetfet scanner. (b) A handheld scanner. (c) A flatbed scanner.

software to actually "read," or decipher, individual characters or digits. For example, the U.S. Postal Service scans addresses on mail using optical character recognition to read each address and send the mail on its way.

8 bits = 1 byte

Processing Hardware

Data   Computers don't understand what letters of the alphabet or punctuation marks are. Computers only understand zeros and ones. Data is represented in the computer as 1s (ones) and 0s (zeros). For example, when you type the letter A on the keyboard the computer actually "sees" the data as **01000001**. That's eight zeros and ones in a very specific sequence. If you were to type the letter B, the computer would actually recognize the data as **01000010**. Notice that the letter B uses yet a different sequence of zeros and ones. In fact, every single character on the keyboard has its own unique sequence of zeros and ones.

These zeros and ones are called **bits**. The term bit is simply and abbreviation for **bi**nary dig**its**. Each character is represented by a unique sequence of eight bits. Each eight-bit sequence of bits is called a byte. A byte is roughly equivalent to one character of data such as a letter, a number, or a special character. Computers (regardless of their brand) can share data with one another because they use the same coding structure (of eight bits) for each character. This coding structure is called the **American Standard Code for Information Interchange (ASCII)**.

When you work on a computer, you manipulate data in the form of files. A **file** is a block of bytes making up either a computer program or computer data. Each file must be given a unique name. Your work will involve creating data files such as letters, reports, financial models, pictures, sounds, and so forth. Usually computer files are made up of thousands if not millions of bytes of data. Computer storage and memory capacities are measured according to the number of bytes of data that can be stored in them. Computer processing performance is measured according to the number of bytes that can be processed in a given amount of time.

The term **kilo** (usually referred to simply as **K**) refers to the number 1,000. Actually, one **kilobyte (KB)** of data actually refers to 1,024, but we usually simply think of the stored data in the round number of 1,000 bytes. Thus, 580KB or 580K is 580 kilobytes or approximately 580,000 characters. The

term **mega**, or **M**, refers to approximately one million. So the quantity **4MB** refers to approximately 4 million bytes. The term **giga**, or **G,** is an amount roughly equivalent to 1 billion, and the term **tera**, or **T**, is roughly equivalent to 1 trillion.

> **FYI**   These Numbers Are Significant.
>
> Sometimes it is difficult to comprehend the size of very large numbers. To understand how significant these numbers are, consider the passage of time. Everyone knows that there are 60 seconds in a minute and 60 minutes in an hour. But did you know that there are 86,400 seconds in one day, 604,800 seconds in a week, 2.5 million seconds in a month, and 32 million seconds in one year? Amazingly, for a billion seconds to pass it takes roughly 32 years. For a trillion seconds to pass, it takes 32,000 years! So when we talk about storage and processing capacities for microcomputers in the millions, billions, and trillions, we're talking about numbers of significance!

After data is input, it is processed. Processing hardware consists of the central processing unit and primary storage (RAM, ROM, and the data bus). A microcomputer uses one chip as its CPU and multiple chips as primary storage. A chip is a small, rectangular piece of silicon—an element extracted from sand—that contains thousands, perhaps millions, of circuits.

The fifth basic principle of computers is that all computers (regardless of their classification) can perform three basic functions. These three basic functions are **arithmetic operations, logical comparisons, and storage and retrieval**.

All computers are capable of performing addition, subtraction, multiplication, and division—no more, no less. The arithmetic operations that a computer can perform are no different than basic arithmetic that is taught in elementary school. The primary difference is that the computer can perform these calculations with lighting quick speed.

All computers are also capable of performing six logical comparisons. These logical comparisons are greater than, less than, equal to, not equal to, greater than or equal to, and less than or equal to.

Imagine a balance scale and you will understand that the logical comparisons are not more complex than most humans learn at a very early age.

These arithmetic operations and logical comparisons are performed in an area of the *central processing unit (CPU)* called the *arithmetic and logic unit (ALU)*.

CPU. The brain of PC.

The Central Processing Unit

The central processing unit (CPU) is often called the brain of the computer because the CPU interprets and executes program instructions.

In a microcomputer, the CPU is called a *microprocessor*. If you take a computer apart and look inside, the microprocessor will have a plastic casing, such as the one labeled in Figure 12. In this case, an Intel Pentium microprocessor is located inside the plastic casing. Surrounding the CPU on the main circuit board are many supporting computer chips.

Intel Corporation controls a large part of the microprocessor market for IBM and compatible microcomputers. Motorola, AMD, and Cyrix also design and manufacture microprocessors for personal computers.

An important characteristic of a CPU is how many bits of data it can process at one time. The more bits processed in an instant, the faster the CPU. The CPU found in the original Apple II computer, a Motorola microprocessor, could process only eight bits at a time. Think of it as an eight-lane highway. However, the CPU in the original IBM PC, the Intel 8088, could process 16 bits (like a 16-lane highway). With these CPUs, large numbers must be broken down into smaller parts before they can be processed, which greatly slows down the CPU.

CPUs such as the Intel 80386 and the Intel 80486 were much faster because they could manipulate 32 bits at a time, which meant that large numbers (and more data) could be processed in a single action. A feature that makes the Intel Pentium so powerful (see Figure 12) is its advanced super-scalar design, which enables it to process two 32-bit instructions at one time. Most computer manufacturers currently are placing only Intel Pentium, or Intel Pentium-compatible CPUs (CPUs made by companies such as Cyrix or AMD) in their computers. It's important to get the fastest CPU you can afford.

Figure 12 In this photo, the protective covering has been cut away to reveal the superfine wires connecting the actual microchip to the casing package.

The Pentium II microprocessor was built on the design of the Pentium Pro, but added an additional 2 million transistors to bring the total up to 7.5 million. Intel's newest Pentium II microprocessor is called Deschutes. Unlike previous Pentium IIs manufactured with a 0.35-micron process, the Deschutes processors have transistor sizes of 0.25 microns. The smaller size will enable Intel to produce smaller chips with lower power consumption.

Another distinguishing characteristic of a CPU is its *clock speed*, the speed at which the computer's internal clock synchronizes computer operations. Like a metronome or an orchestra conductor that keeps musicians in time with the music, a tiny quartz crystal inside the CPU emits electrical pulses that determine how quickly the CPU will execute instructions. In general, the more pulses per second that the crystal emits, the faster the CPU can perform. One pulse per second is referred to as one *hertz*. Typically, computers run at many millions of pulses per second, so they have a clock speed measured in *megahertz (MHz)*. The CPU in the original IBM PC ran at 4.77 megahertz, or about 5 million pulses per second. Current versions of the Pentium II chip run at speeds of up to 333 MHz. The first of the Deschutes chips run at 333 MHz. Chips at 350 MHz and faster are expected.

The CPU clock speed that you need in your computer will be determined by what kind of applications you are using. Simple text entry using a word processor does not require a particularly fast computer. Applications that are CPU intensive, however, such as graphics or multimedia programs, are worth the extra financial investment in a computer with a higher clock speed. Again, it's important to get the fastest CPU you can afford.

Memory

Random-Access Memory **Random-access memory (RAM)**, sometimes called main memory or primary storage, holds data and instructions for processing in small components called RAM chips. You can consider RAM to be a temporary work area in which you use application software to refine data until the data is in its completed form. For example, when you type correspondence using a program such as a word processor, both the word processing program and the data making up the correspondence are *temporarily* contained in the computer's RAM chips. When you complete the document, you can print it, but if you turn off the computer, the letter will disappear from the RAM chips. Because RAM is temporary, it is important to save any work that you plan to use again. In fact, it is very important that you understand the volatility of RAM. If the power to the computer system is disrupted, even for a moment, the data and instructions held in the RAM chips will disappear! So you should learn how to save your data to a more permanent secondary storage device (such as a diskette or hard disk drive).

RAM is what gives microcomputers their multipurpose nature. Today's microcomputers are very powerful computing devices that are capable of many different functions and many concurrent functions (called **multitasking**). Microcomputers typically come with 16, 32, or even 64 megabytes of memory capacity in RAM chips. The more RAM you have, the more memory you'll have for programs and data. Choose the amount of RAM based on the applications you will be running. For example, if you want to run multiple programs simultaneously in Microsoft Windows, you will want as much RAM as you can afford. This is an important consideration. Remember that all computer instructions must be interpreted (for the computer) as 1s and 0s. In order for us humans to not be required to communicate by typing in 1s and 0s, we need a lot of room in RAM for our computer interface.

Figure 13 shows a **single in-line memory module (SIMM)**, of which the RAM in most computers is

Figure 13 A SIMM (Single In-line Memory Module).

made. Typically, PCs use nine-chip SIMMs and Macintoshes use eight-chip SIMMs. To add RAM, you can take the cover off the computer and plug additional SIMMs into special memory slots. SIMMs are available at most computer stores.

Many newer computers utilize DIMM chips for memory. Dimm is short for Dual In-line Memory Module, a small circuit board that holds memory chips. A single in-line memory module (SIMM) has a 32-bit path to the memory chips, whereas a DIMM has a 64-bit path. Because the Pentium processor requires a 64-bit path to memory, you need to install SIMMs two at a time. With DIMMs, you can install memory one DIMM at a time. However, DIMMs are currently more expensive than SIMMs.

Read-Only Memory **Read-only memory (ROM)** is another type of computer memory that contains data and programs, but unlike RAM, the contents of ROM do not disappear when you turn off the computer. The programs in ROM are stored on the ROM chips by the manufacturer before you buy the computer. On the main circuit board, ROM chips contain a wide variety of diagnostic software that checks the computer's hardware each time you turn the computer on. If there is a faulty component, the ROM software will detect it and describe the problem on the screen. One of the last things ROM does at startup is load operating system software into RAM so you can begin using the computer. Many other special function ROM chips on the main circuit board also control the computer's functions.

The Data Bus Data must flow from the CPU to Ram and other components of the computer system. The microscopic "roadways" that carry the data are called the **data busses**. These data busses vary in width (like a multilane highway) depending on which type of CPU the computer is equipped with. The original IBM PC had an eight-bit data bus (like an eight-lane highway). The Intel 80386SX microprocessor could process data 32 bits at a time but the data were only 16 bit. This created a bottleneck when the data flowed from the CPU into the data bus (like squeezing 32 lanes of traffic into a sixteen-lane highway).

The Intel Pentium processor has a 32-bit data bus for each instruction being executed. Remember that because of its superscalar design, which can execute two 32-bit instructions simultaneously, in effect a Pentium has a 64-bit data bus.

Output Hardware

The two most common types of output devices, **visual displays** and **printers**, are ideally suited for outputting words, numbers, and graphics to the human user of the computer system. As you type characters, those characters appear on the display screen. When you want the characters on a sheet of paper, you simply direct the computer system to print the characters on a printer.

Computer output is classified as either **soft-copy** output or **hard-copy** output. Hard-copy output is tangible and permanent. Printing on some type of physical media such as paper usually produces hard-copy output. Soft-copy output is produced in a non-permanent form and usually displayed temporarily on some type of visual display device.

Screen Output   Visual display screens, also called **monitors**, are the most prominent output devices for computers. Monitors vary in how they produce their images, either through TV-style technology or flat panel designs.

Most desktop computer systems use TV-style **cathode ray tube (CRT)** screens. In a color CRT, three electron-beams—one for each primary color (red, green, and blue)—shoot out at the phosphor on the front of the picture tube to illuminate tiny dots called pixels. **Pixel** is short for **picture element**. The three beams—one red, one green, and one blue **(RGB)**—each vary in intensity to create any color of the rainbow. 映像点.

The total number of pixels and the distance between pixels defines screen resolution, which is the sharpness of the picture image. The more dots that make up a picture and the closer the dots are

FYI   Resolution Is Key.

Consider the video display units used to display replays at many stadiums. The displays typically struggle to display images with any significant detail because the dots (pixels) used to create the images are so large. It's not uncommon for the pixels on a stadium scoreboard to be the physical size of a softball, and the separation between the dots (dot pitch) is measured in inches rather than millimeters.

to one another, the better the quality of the image and the higher its resolution. The **video graphics array (VGA)** standard can display 640 pixels across by 480 pixels down. The **super VGA (SVGA)** is defined as up to 1,024 pixels by 768 pixels. Obviously, SVGA can produce a finer visual image than standard VGA. The **dot pitch (dp)**, which is the distance between pixels, is measured in millimeters (mm). Dot pitch of .28mm is fairly common, and dot pitch higher than .28 (.32, .39) provides a lower quality image. Dot pitch of less than .28 will provide a higher quality image but this higher quality means higher price.

CRTs are excellent video displays for high-resolution images and desktop systems. Portable computer designers, however, have found it difficult to use CRTs because of their size, weight, and high power consumption. A good alternative to the CRT is the **liquid crystal display (LCD)**. In a LCD panel, liquid crystal is sandwiched between two glass plates. Transistors produce electrical charges that darken points in the liquid crystal to create pixels. The pixels are combined to create characters or graphical images on the flat panel screen. LCDs are flat, lightweight, and consume little electrical power, all of which makes them well suited for portable computers. Figure 14 shows a variety of visual display devices.

Significant research is being done on LCDs to improve their resolution, increase their size, and lower their cost. New large-size flat panel displays are being released based on gas-plasma technology; this technology is still fairly expensive, however.

Printer Output   Unlike soft-copy output, which is displayed on a video display device, printers produce hard-copy output, which is tangible and perma-

Figure 14 A variety of display screens. (a) A super VGA (SVGA) CRT is best for high-resolution needs. (b) Monochrome displays are used in text-based applications where no color is needed. (c) LCD screens are particularly useful in portable computers.

nent. Printers fit into two basic groups: ***nonimpact*** printers and ***impact*** printers. Nonimpact printers produce output with lasers or tiny drops of ink. They are typically more expensive than impact printers (although that is changing) and generally produce better-quality output.

Figure 15 shows a ***laser printer***, which uses technology similar to that used in photocopy machines. Laser printers are superb for creating hard-copy images quickly and quietly. As shown in Figure 16, a laser printer shoots a beam on a positively charged, rotating drum to create characters and

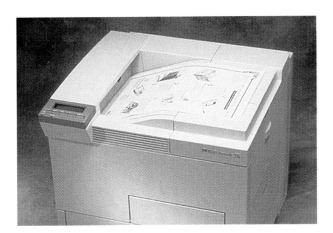

Figure 15 Hewlett-Packard leads the laser printer market because of the durability of their printers and the company's ability to continually produce very high-quality output.

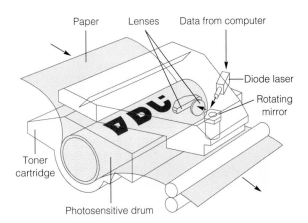

Figure 16 A laser printer uses technology very similar to that used in a copy machine. Text and images are created using patterns of tiny dots.

graphical images out of tiny dots. These dot images become neutralized and then roll by toner (usually black) emitted from a toner cartridge. The toner sticks to the neutralized areas and then is deposited on a sheet of paper. Finally, the paper and toner are heated to permanently fuse them together.

Like video displays, the quality of nonimpact printers is measured in how many dots make up the image (as measured per inch). The *resolution* of laser printer output typically ranges from 300 to 600 dots per inch (dpi). Remember that the more dots (in the same space) that make up a printed character or image, the higher the resolution and the better the output quality. Because dpi can be measured in square inches on hard-copy printers, a 300 dpi printer actually creates its printed output with 90,000 dots per square inch (300 × 300). A 600 dpi printer is not twice the resolution of a 300 dpi printer. At 360,000 dots per square inch (600 × 600) it is actually four times the resolution! At these resolutions, unlike the characters created by a dot matrix printer, laser printer characters have dots visible only with a magnifying glass. Color laser printers exist and will become common due to continually decreasing costs.

Figure 17 shows an *ink-jet printer*, which shoots drops of ink onto paper and is just as quiet as a laser printer. The print head sprays ink from multiple nozzles to create characters out of dots, in patterns similar to those created by a dot matrix printer. Ink-jet resolution is often as high as that of a low- to mid-range laser printer, and most ink-jet printers are capable of printing in color. Ink-jet printers capable of printing color images at resolutions of 600 dpi (or higher) are not uncommon. Although they tend to be slow, ink-jet printers produce high-quality output and can sell for a fraction of the price of laser printers.

Impact printers, similar to typewriters, physically strike the paper. The most common type of impact printer is the dot matrix printer, which creates characters by using small dots. A print head contains 9 to 24 tiny hammers, or pins, that strike the print ribbon, which then hits the paper to produce the dots that make up the characters. Better resolution is obtained by either having more pins or performing multiple passes across the paper. The final printout can contain text, graphics, or a combination of the two. Dot matrix printers are relatively inexpensive, even cheaper than ink jet printers, but tend to be loud and slow.

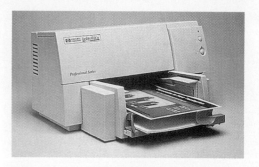

Figure 17 Color ink-jet printers are very popular for personal computing due to their affordability and high-quality output.

The letter **G** shown in Figure 18 was created as a 5 by 7 matrix of dots on a 9-pin printer. All the characters shown in the figure were created by dots as the print head swept across the paper. All of these characters use only the top seven pins. The bottom two pins are used to underline characters or to create the lower parts of the lowercase letters g, j, p, and y (not shown in Figure 18). Impact printers are still important in that they are required to print on multiple part (carbonless) forms. To successfully transfer from the top page to the succeeding pages in a multiple part form, an actual impact must be made with the paper. The heavier the pressure on the top sheet, the better the transfer will be to the underlying sheets. Nonimpact printers cannot successfully print on multiple part forms in that they only "paint" the top sheet.

Storage Hardware   *permanent.*

Long-term storage, or *secondary storage*, refers to nonvolatile data storage devices that are separate from primary memory (RAM) chips. Because data in secondary storage does not disappear when the computer is turned off, you can use secondary storage to store work more permanently. The two most common forms of secondary storage are *magnetic disks* and *magnetic tapes*. Data is stored by changing the magnetic field on the iron oxide that coats the surface of both disks and tapes. Remember that computers can only understand 1s and 0s. In magnetic storage media, the presence of a magnetic spot represents a one and the absence of a magnetic spot is equivalent to a zero. Devices called *disk drives* control disks, and *tape drives* control tapes.

Floppy Disks   *Floppy disks,* sometimes called *diskettes,* are round (inside a square case) and

9
pins.

Figure 18 The dot matrix printing process and some sample output.

聚脂薄膜.

made of a flexible material called *Mylar* in the form of a disk. Since Mylar (plastic) cannot be magnetized or demagnetized, the plastic disk is covered with an iron oxide coating that can be magnetized and demagnetized. Floppy disks come in two sizes, 3½ inches and 5¼ inches. Floppy disks also come in two densities, low-density and high-density. Both sizes are housed in a square plastic case; the 3½-inch case is rigid whereas the 5¼-inch case is flexible. The 5¼-inch disks are not used much in today's microcomputers, but 3½-inch disks (called microfloppy diskettes) are still very prevalent. The term floppy disk usually refers to both the Mylar disk and the plastic case. Floppy disks can be removed from a computer's floppy-disk drive and easily transported. For example, if you use a home computer to create a document, you can store the document on a floppy disk and then take that disk to work or school to edit or print the document. The following table summarizes floppy-disk densities and memory capacities for floppy disks used in PCs.

If indeed today's microfloppy (3½-inch) diskette can store over eleven million magnetic spots (bits), then clearly the magnetic spots that are placed on floppy disks are very tiny. With that in mind, it is important to be careful with floppy disks in order to safeguard your valuable data. Magnets can destroy data on disks; even magnets found in speakers and microphones can damage data on a floppy disk.

Direct sunlight can warp the plastic case, making the data unreadable.

Hard Disks **Hard disks** usually have a much higher storage capacity than floppy disks. Most hard disk drives are made with at least a one-gigabyte storage capacity and these larger hard disk drives are readily available. A hard disk is typically made of rigid aluminum platters (a newer technology uses glass)

3 1/2-Inch Floppy Diskettes

	Bytes	Bits	Single-spaced pages of text
Low Density	720 K	5,760,000	150
High Density	1.44 M	11,520,000	300

5 1/4-Inch Floppy Diskettes

	Bytes	Bits	Single-spaced pages of text
Low Density	360 K	2,880,000	75
High Density	1.2 M	9,600,000	250

on which data can be packed much more closely than on a floppy disk. Again, because aluminum (and glass) cannot be magnetized and demagnetized, the rigid disks are covered with an iron oxide coating. Because the data is so tightly packed and because hard disks spin at least ten times faster than floppy disks, you can access data on hard disks much faster than data on floppies. Hard disks are also more reliable, as they are completely sealed in the hard disk drive, which cannot be easily removed from the computer.

The **read/write head** is a small magnet that reads and writes data on a disk. On a floppy disk, the read/write head drags on the disk surface; on a hard disk, the read/write head floats above the disk surface. If a read/write head were to touch the surface of a hard disk platter at 3,600 revolutions per minute (the speed of a table saw), the read/write head would scrape off the iron oxide coating (and the magnetized spots) rendering the data unreadable. We call this problem a "head crash" and many head crashes are caused by moving a computer system while the hard disk drive is actively spinning (which is anytime the computer is on). Figure 19 shows a hard disk drive with its outside cover removed. The read/write head is at the end of the access arm. Shaking

a computer when the hard disk is reading or writing data can cause the read/write head to crash into the surface and possibly destroy data.

Another type of head crash results from a foreign particle getting stuck between the read/write head and the disk surface. The read/write head floats at less than 5/1,000,000 of an inch above the disk surface. This distance is smaller than a smoke particle, dust particle, fingerprint, or human hair, as shown in Figure 20. This type of head crash is rare, because hard disk drives are hermetically sealed to keep foreign particles from entering the disk platter compartment.

Hard disks typically consist of a stack of aluminum platters like those shown in Figure 21. All platters have access arms above and below each disk surface with a read/write head mounted on the end of each arm. The access arms (and read/write heads) move in unison back and forth over the surface of the disk depending on where the data is stored on the disk.

Both floppy and hard disks store data in **tracks**, which are concentric circles on the surface of a disk, as shown in Figure 22. Tracks are laid out on a disk when the disk is **formatted** or **initialized** (prepared for use). One side of a floppy disk contains 40 to 80 tracks depending on the density; a hard disk can have 600 or more tracks. Tracks are then divided into **sectors** (wedges), which are always 512

Figure 19 A hard disk drive for a personal computer. The inside of a 3½-inch hard disk with the top access arm and read/write head visible.

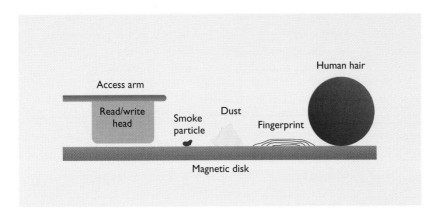

Figure 20 The read/write head flies very close to the surface of the hard disk platter. If the head encounters even the smallest particle, the disk will be damaged and important data can be destroyed.

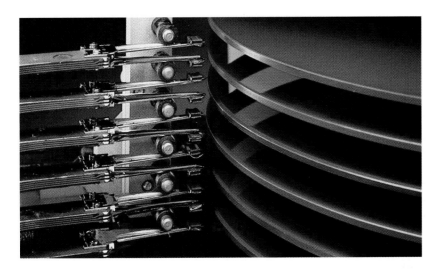

Figure 21 Read/write heads and access arms. A read/write head is on the end of each access arm. An access arm and a read/write head are above and below each disk platter.

Track 399

Track 000

Figure 22 The magnetic tracks on a disk used to provide a system for storing and retrieving data.

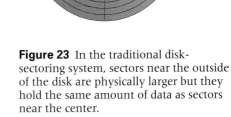

Sector

Hard Disk

Store data in tracks

Tracks

bytes long on both floppy and hard disks (see Figure 23). This track and sector system provides a two-dimensional system whereby the computer can keep track of where data is stored on each disk surface. Unformatted disks have no tracks or sectors, and therefore cannot store any data.

Disk access time is a measure of the time that it takes to find the track and then the sector that contains desired data. Manufacturers seldom advertise a floppy disk drive's average access time because it is always slow, more than 100 ms (*milliseconds*, or

Figure 23 In the traditional disk-sectoring system, sectors near the outside of the disk are physically larger but they hold the same amount of data as sectors near the center.

thousandths of a second). Hard disk drive average access times, which are typically 15 ms or less, are important because they play a significant role in determining how fast software is loaded from the hard disk to the computer's RAM.

Magnetic Tape Magnetic tape used in computers is similar to tape used in home tape recorders and is especially well suited for making backup copies of large amounts of data. The tape is made of Mylar and is wound on reels a couple of inches wide. Reels are contained in plastic cassettes as small as the ones used for taping speech and music. Although data access on magnetic tape is much slower than on disk, it is less expensive. Because a tape can store one gigabyte or more at a very low cost, companies typically back up important data onto magnetic tape on a daily or weekly basis. Figure 24 shows a few of the varieties of magnetic tape.

Other Magnetic Media There are companies (such as SyQuest Technology, Inc. and Iomega Corporation) that design, manufacture, and market innovative, high-performance, removable (and patented) data storage solutions that help personal computer users manage their data in a portable fashion. These data storage solutions can store from 100 MB to 5 GB of data. Figure 25 shows a 100-megabyte zip disk drive made by Iomega.

CD-ROM Whereas floppy and hard disks use magnetic technology, CDs (compact disks) use optical (laser) technology. A ***compact disk-read-only memory (CD-ROM)*** drive is an optical disk drive that uses lasers to read microscopic cavities in CD-ROMs. Although they are not as fast at retrieving data as hard disk drives, CD-ROM drives can read data that is packed much more tightly in a comparable amount of space. One 12-centimeter (4¼-inch) CD-ROM can hold up to 680 megabytes of data. This means that the typical CD-ROM stores over 5.4 billion 1s and 0s equaling over 130,000 single-spaced typed pages of text. However, CD-ROMs are capable of so much more. In addition to standard text-based data storage, CD-ROMs can

include animation, video clips, graphics, and sound. With these capabilities, CD-ROMs offer computer users true multimedia-oriented interactive applications (such as encyclopedias, tutorials, games, etc.).

A CD-ROM consists of a thin sheet of aluminum sandwiched between one layer of plastic and one layer of lacquer (see Figure 26). The laser penetrates the plastic side to read *pits*, tiny cavities, and *lands*, small flat areas, in the aluminum. Pits and lands, a record of 1s and 0s used to define data, are arranged in a long spiral that starts on the outside of the disk and winds its way to the center. This long strand of data is roughly three miles long from beginning to end.

The aluminum under the plastic of a CD-ROM is unalterable—hence the label CD-ROM, as in "read only." Once data is written, it cannot be modified or erased; therefore, CD-ROMs are used to complement hard disk drives, not replace them. Typically, software companies will fill CD-ROMs with programs, clip art, the works of Shakespeare, or entire encyclopedias. CD-ROM encyclopedias can contain photographs and animation, as well as video and sound clips.

A typical CD-ROM drive locates data on a compact disk at between 200 and 300 milliseconds, which is very slow compared to hard disk access times of less than 15 milliseconds. With a hard disk, quick access time is important because related data is often scattered across the disk in many different locations. Because CD-ROM drives tend to read long streams of related data from adjacent areas, how fast the CD-ROM drive finds data is not quite as important as the data transfer rate, the speed at which the data is read from the disk. Early CD-ROM drives transferred data at 150 kilobytes per second. This speed was called 1X, which was equivalent to the same speed as audio CD players.

(a)

(b)

(c)

Figure 24 (a) Tape cartridges. (b) A magnetic tape cassette. (c) A digital audiotape (DAT).

Figure 25 A removable secondary storage device.

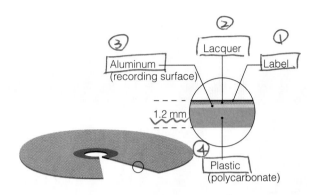

Figure 26 A cross-section of a CD-ROM.

At such a slow speed, video clips appeared jerky, because the video data was not transferred to the screen quickly enough. The double-speed drive (2X) was then created, transferring data at 300 kilobytes per second, at which speed the video clips ran more smoothly. Emerging standards include 24X, which is 3,600 kilobytes per second. Of course, these very fast CD-ROMs can automatically slow themselves down to 1X speed if an audio CD is placed in the CD-ROM drive.

In a typical computer lab environment, like the ones found in most colleges and universities, applications software is usually stored on hard disks and the data students create is stored on floppy disks (or some other type of portable storage media). So if you are using a software package such as a word processor in a lab environment, you will probably not need to buy the actual product, because it has been loaded onto the lab computer's hard disk. You will need a floppy disk (or some other type of portable storage media as specified by your instructor) to store your documents, projects, and other data. Although you could store your work on the hard disk, most computer labs don't want student data files filling up their hard disks. More and more schools are also using CD-ROM drives. These, of course, are just for reading programs and data.

*CD-R   **Recordable CDs (CD-Rs)*** offer computer users a versatile, cost-effective solution for data archiving, information distribution, and multimedia publishing. In some units (like the Hewlett-Packard SureStore) both the drive and the media use revolutionary new CD-RW (**ReW**ritable) technology. If the drives comply with industry standards they can enable easy drag-and-drop file transfer from a hard

drive to the CD. The new CD-R drives allow computer users to create permanent archives and distribute files to millions of CD-ROM and audio players worldwide. These CD-Rs offer universal compatibility with regular CD-ROM drives to store over 650 MB or 74 minutes of audio per disc. CD-Rs allow users to erase and rewrite information up to 1,000 times per sector per disc with permanent stability and 100-year shelf life.

*DVD   **Digital versatile disks (DVDs)*** offer expanded storage capacity of CD-ROMs in that they can easily store twice as much and even more. DVDs can store more data because the size of the pits (cavities that represent 1s) is only half the size of the pits on standard CD-ROMs. Because of newer technologies that can pack more and more data in the same physical space, single-sided DVDs can store 4.7 gigabytes or 133 minutes of full motion video and CD-quality sound. Double-sided DVDs are capable of storing 9.4 GB or 266 minutes of video and audio. Initial DVD drives are read-only drives but recordable DVD drives are not far off. DVD technology is poised to truly revolutionize secondary storage and the applications that we run on computers.

Computer Interface Ports

Most computers come with a variety of ports that are available to plug in cables (and peripheral devices). The different types of ports that come on computers have different capabilities and are used to connect the computer system to a variety of devices (see Figure 27). Your computer may be equipped with ***parallel, serial,*** or ***SCSI interface ports*** (or perhaps all three).

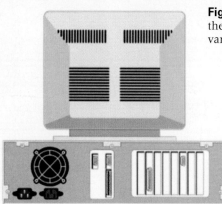

Figure 27 Interface ports are usually located the back of the computer system and are used to connect a wide variety of devices to the computer.

Communications Hardware

Data communications hardware has become essential for today's computers. Data communications devices can be your telecommunications link to the outside world. Computers can communicate over telephone lines or via cables that directly connect one computer to another (as in a computer network).

Often, new computers come with a built-in modem that enables you to send electronic mail, connect to university computer systems, and/or on-line services. For a more complete discussion of the services available over phone lines, see the section titled "Commercial Information Services" later in this book.

Crosstalk problem ∴ 10 fts.

8 times faster

Parallel The *parallel interface port* is an all-purpose interface port that can be used to attach printers, tape drives, video cameras, and so forth to your computer. With a parallel interface port, data moves eight bits at a time (imagine this as eight cars moving in parallel down an eight-lane highway). Unfortunately, data *crosstalk* becomes a problem the longer the distance of the interface. Data crosstalk occurs when data bits "cross over" from one "lane" to another. Because data crosstalk becomes significant in parallel interfaces as the length grows, most parallel connections are limited to ten feet in length. Some parallel connections can extend up to twenty feet provided that specially built cables are used.

no Crosstalk problem ∴ lengthy.

Serial The *serial interface port* is also an all-purpose interface port that can be used to attach pointing devices (such as joysticks and trackballs), modems, and occasionally printers, to your computer. With a serial interface port, data moves one bit at a time (in one channel). Because data moves through serial interfaces in "single file," data crosstalk does not become a problem when the connection distance increases. With this in mind, the length of serial connections can be quite lengthy. However, the standard serial interface is, of course, eight times slower than the standard parallel interface.

SCSI The *small computer systems interface (SCSI)* is a very fast and highly versatile, all-purpose interface port that can be used to attach a wide variety of devices (disk drives, CD ROMs, scanners, and so forth) to the computer. One single SCSI port on the back of a computer can be used to attach up to seven different devices simultaneously. Because SCSI interfaces are very fast and are highly versatile, they add to the overall price of the computer system, but their value can be well worth the added cost.

Modems Before data can be transmitted over phone lines, the data must be converted from its original *digital* signal, the signal computers use, to an *analog* signal, the signal that can be transmitted over telephone lines. Digital signals consist of electrical pulses that represent bits (1s and 0s). A pulse indicates a 1; the absence of a pulse indicates a 0. Bits are usually placed together in groups of eight to create bytes, each of which can be thought of as being roughly equivalent to a character. For example, in most computers, **01000001** represents the letter A. The digital signal for **01000001** has a time sequence in which there is an absence of a pulse (**0**), a pulse (**1**), five time sequences in which a pulse is absent (**00000**), and then one pulse (**1**).

Most of today's telephone lines are designed to carry analog signals, not digital signals. Your voice is a good example of an analog signal. When you speak, you do not blurt out pulses at exacting intermittent intervals. Your words flow in a continuous stream of sound. To be transmitted over phone lines, digital pulses must be converted into two sounds, one that represents a 1 and one that represents a 0. A *modem*, or **mo**dulator/**dem**odulator, is found at each end of a two-computer telecommunications system. The modem of the source computer *modulates,* or translates, the digital signal into an analog signal; the modem at the target computer *demodulates*, or translates, the analog signal back into digital signal. The two modems carry on a two-way "conversation" alternately modulating and demodulating each other's signals (see Figure 28). Styles of modems can be either *internal* (located inside the computer) or *external* (placed outside the computer). Both types of modems have cables that connect them to a telephone line. Figure 29 shows an internal modem and an external modem.

When buying a modem, you will encounter an array of communications terms and concepts. The most important term is bps, which refers to the

Figure 28 Modems are used to convert (modulate) digital data signals to analog signals for transport over telecommunications lines. Then the modem on the other end of the transmission reverses the process (demodulates) by converting the analog signals back to digital data signals.

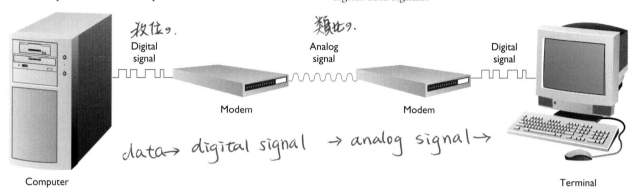

数位の.
Digital signal

類比の.
Analog signal

Digital signal

Modem

Modem

data→ digital signal → analog signal→

Computer

Terminal

(a)

(b)

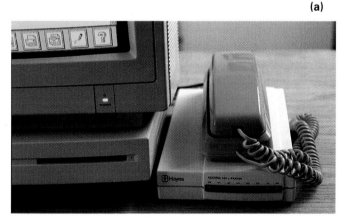

Figure 29
(a) An external modem.
(b) An internal modem.

speed at which data is transmitted. The higher the bps rate the faster the data travels. Older modems carry data at 9,600 or 14,400 bps. Newer modems have transmission speeds of 28,800, 33,600, or even 56,000 bps. Figure 30 shows the time it would take to transfer a twenty-page report at the different transfer rates.

With a computer equipped with a telephone modem, you can connect with and exchange data with colleagues, access remote computers from home, use on-line information services, use bulletin board systems, and access the Internet. With today's graphical user interfaces on computer systems and the graphical look and feel of the on-line communications, it is important to equip your home computer with the fastest communications hardware that you can afford.

Rate (bps)	Time to transmit a 20-page single-spaced report
1,200	10 minutes
2,400	5 minutes
9,600	1.25 minutes
14,400	50 secods
28,800	25 seconds
33,600	30 seconds
56,000	12.5 seconds

Figure 30 Data transfer rates compared.

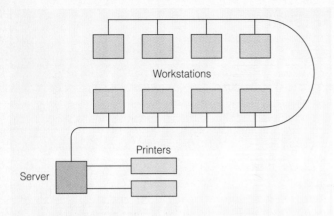

Figure 31 A typical layout of a computer network.

Network Interface Cards Figure 31 shows a computer **network**, which is a collection of computers that are connected together. Networks are groups of computers that are linked together to "talk." There are many reasons to network computers together. One reason is to enable multiple computers to share peripheral devices such as expensive printers, scanners, and CD-ROM drives. Another reason to network computers is to allow people to exchange messages and easily transfer data files with one another. A third reason to network is to enable computer users to effectively collaborate so that, for example, three people in different departments can write a report together, or work with the same spreadsheet. This shared information capability is particularly useful in the case of shared databases (like the database that your university registrar uses to track student grades) that may need to be accessed and modified by many people simultaneously in an organization.

Computer networks are designed to "link" two or more computers together. These "linkages" can take many forms. The most common form of linking computers together is through physical data cabling. These data linkages use either *copper-based cabling* or *fiber optic based cables.*

Copper cabling is the most prevalent type of network cable used. Each pair of copper cables is capable of carrying one data or one voice transmission. This capability is called the network's carrying capacity. Unfortunately, copper cabling degrades over time (particularly when exposed to moisture) and copper is a nonrenewable resource. As supplies diminish, copper becomes more and more expensive.

Fiber optic based cabling is growing in use. Each hair-thin strand of glass fiber (see Figure 32) is capable of handling over 4,000 simultaneous data or voice transmissions! Fiber optic cabling does not degrade over time and is impervious to water. Because the cable is made of glass, the raw material is silicon or sand. This renewable resource keeps prices very low for fiber optic cabling. Perhaps the biggest advantage of fiber optic cabling is that data is transmitted as pulse of light (at the speed of light). Because data doesn't have to be modified from digital to analog and back (light pulses are digital), the data doesn't have to go through the slow process of modulating and demodulating.

Figure 32 Fiber optic cable. Light is transmitted through hair-thin fiber optic strands.

Many computing environments (such as college campuses) are networked. Typically a fairly powerful computer called a *server* is loaded with various applications software and connected to a variety of networked peripheral devices (such as printers or scanners). The server offers its services to any authorized computer attached to the computer network. From a local computer, or **workstation**, you can access programs and share data on the hard disk located in the central server computer. After you are finished creating a document (file), you can print the document on one of the server's shared printers or on your local printer.

A local computer is connected to the network through a **network interface card (NIC)** like the one shown in Figure 33. This circuit board, which plugs into the computer, serves as an interface between

Figure 33 A network interface card.

the local computer and the network. Most network interface cards (NICs) are capable of transmitting data at either ten megabits per second or 100 megabits per second.

Some networks are self-contained. Users can share programs and data within the network, but not with the outside world (unless the network is designed and built to connect to the outside world). However, the current trend is for networks to be connected with other networks via either a modem or direct cable connections. For more on networks, see the section titled "Computer Networking" later in this book.

Software

The main categories of software are *operating system software, application software, communication software,* and *programming languages.* Operating software serves the computer's needs by supervising and controlling the operations of the computer system. Application software serves the human's needs by performing specific people-related tasks, such as writing a term paper, developing a budget, or charting profits. Communications software enables computers to "talk" to other computers and share information. Programming languages are used to write step-by-step instructions for a computer, called computer programs.

Operating Systems

An operating system is a set of programs that enables a computer to manage the input, processing, output, and secondary storage devices that are assembled to make the overall computer system. The operating system also interacts between you and the computer, communicating in a language that the machine understands. Remember that all computer instructions must be given to the computer system in the form of 1s and 0s. At one point in early computer history, all instructions were given by physically "hard wiring" connections inside the computer. Each connection represented a 1. Each nonconnection represented a 0. In later computer history, computers were instructed by flipping small levers, called switches, either on or off. You can imagine how difficult it must have been to instruct a computer to do something. For example, to instruct the computer to delete something would require 48 switches being toggled on or off (six characters × eight bits per character). If it were still that difficult to instruct a computer to do a simple task, few of us would be tempted to actually use one. Today's operating systems make it far easier to instruct the computer to carry out tasks. Although you may not think about it much, the operating system is always running in the background, ensuring that the computer operates smoothly and easily.

Operating systems also work hand in hand with application programs to make them easy to use, fast, accurate, and safe. The operating system not only helps you start an application, it then works quietly behind the scenes while the application software is serving you, to perform tasks that are essential to the effective and efficient functioning of the computer system. Operating systems perform many functions that govern the operation of the computer system. They allow you to manage your disks and files by formatting the disks, copying files, renaming files, and erasing files. The operating system also allows you to manage files by setting up directories or folders on the disk to store files in a more organized manner and then displaying a directory of all of the files stored on the disk.

The most popular operating system for IBM PCs and compatibles (first introduced in the fall of 1981) was the Microsoft *disk operating system,* commonly known as *DOS*. Although DOS underwent many changes over the years, its job has remained the same: to supervise and control the basic operations of the computer. For example, when you save a document in a program such as WordPerfect or Lotus 1-2-3, the computer program tells DOS that you want to save your work. DOS, the communicator between the hardware and the application software, finds empty space on the disk you specify and then takes the document from RAM and "writes" the document onto the available disk space (using magnetic spots).

You can also use special DOS commands to perform operations more directly, such as copying data from one disk to another, preparing disks for use, checking disks for errors, and so on. In DOS, all commands have to be typed in at the DOS prompt, which is a marker on the screen (usually something like **C:\>**) that indicates that DOS is ready to accept a command. This type of interface, called a *command-line interface,* requires that the computer user know by memory all desired commands. If you don't know a command, you must look it up in a manual. Figure 34 shows the result of the DOS command **DIR/W**, which lists file names horizontally across the screen. The figure also shows the **WP** command, the command used to start WordPerfect 5.l, a DOS-based word processing application.

Figure 35 shows the result of the **WP** command from Figure 34. WordPerfect for DOS was started and a document called "Databases and Privacy" has been typed. Figures 34 and 35 clearly illustrate that DOS-based computers were not as easy to use as the more graphically oriented systems available today, as we discuss next.

An easier way of communicating with a computer is through an operating system that is based on a *graphical-user interface (GUI)*, which allows users

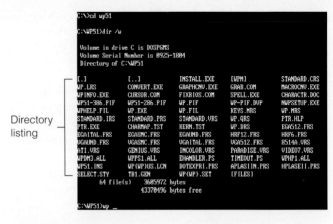

Directory listing

Figure 34 A DOS screen with a directory listing.

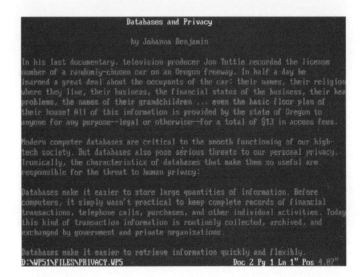

Figure 35 A Wordperfect 5.1 for DOS document screen.

to more easily instruct the computer with pointing devices (such as a mouse or trackball). Most people find the graphical-user interface much easier to use than the DOS command-line interface.

The graphical user interface (GUI) was made popular by the Apple computer corporation with the release of its Macintosh computer in 1984. This shift in the look and feel of the operating system truly revolutionized the computer world. The Macintosh was the first mass-produced computer to feature a graphical user interface. GUIs allowed users to manipulate files, programs, and computer resources by moving *icons,* small graphical representations of elements, with a mouse instead of having to type cryptic commands on a cold, blank screen. In a GUI, a desktop, which is the screen background, serves as a graphics-based work area. Applications and documents appear inside *windows*, rectangular areas on the desktop. Many operations, such as starting an application program, are performed by selecting icons of Windows elements or by choosing commands from **pull-down menus**. In a GUI-based operating system, each icon represents a computer application (such as a word processor), a computer file or document (where data is stored), or a computer resource (such as a hard disk drive or CD-ROM). Through much trial and error, this easy-to-use GUI was not matched on the IBM and IBM PC-compatible platform until 1995 when the Microsoft Corporation released Windows 95. The Macintosh now has a powerful operating system (called System 8, or MacOS). Figure 36 shows several features of the Macintosh screen. Windows now has many of the same features of the Macintosh operating system. Figure 37 shows a typical Windows 98 desktop screen.

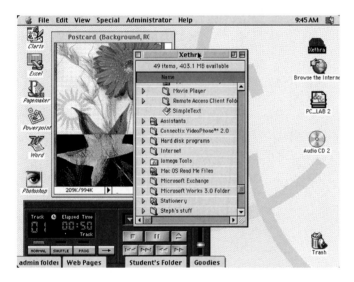

Figure 36 A typical Macintosh screen.

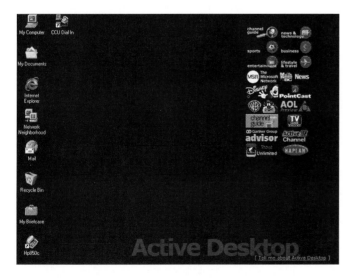

Figure 37 A typical Windows 98 screen.

Applications packages designed for Windows all have the same basic structure and a similar design. For example, the File, Edit, Window, and Help menus are found in almost all Windows-based programs. This consistency among programs greatly simplifies learning new Windows applications.

Windows has sophisticated memory management capabilities that transform DOS from an operating system that could do a single task at a time to a true **multitasking** operating system. A multitasking operating system can run two or more programs simultaneously, with each program running in its own window.

The user whose work appears in Figure 38 was using Microsoft Excel to create a spreadsheet when he realized that he needed to produce a short memo. Without a multitasking system such as Windows, this user would have had to close the first program and then start the second. With Windows, he simply opened another window with Microsoft Word running in it and then typed his memo, without affecting the original spreadsheet file.

Several other operating systems are available for PCs and larger computers. Some PCs run IBM's multitasking GUI operating system called OS/2. UNIX is an operating system for larger computers at many universities, government agencies, and businesses. VMS is an operating system used on many computers created by the Digital Equipment Corporation (DEC).

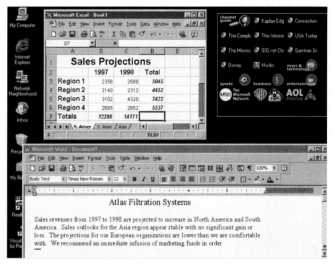

Figure 38 An example of multitasking. Not only are the MS Excel spreadsheet and the MS Word document simultaneously displayed on the screen, but the Windows 98 active desktop is also gathering real-time information from the Internet in the background.

It is important to remember that every computer instruction must still be executed in the form of 1s and 0s inside the computer. So today's GUI operating systems must translate pointer moves and mouse clicks into 1s and 0s that the computer can understand. These operating systems are very sophisticated (from a programming perspective) in order to make them easier to use (from the human perspective). Some of today's operating systems can even translate human speech into computer instructions. As such, operating systems are growing larger all the time. They require more space in the secondary storage of the computer and much more space within the primary memory (RAM) of the computer. Because these newer, easier-to-use operating systems are becoming more sophisticated, they require faster processors to carry out their myriad instructions and translate them into 1s and 0s that the computer can understand. This is why it is so important to have the most powerful PC that you can afford.

Application Software

Most people buy computers to use **application software**. If the operating system software serves the computer's needs, the application software serves the human's needs. The applications that you put on your computer consist of specific "software tools" that you intend to use to make your computer system productive for you. Application software is task specific. Most application software is categorized by the function it performs. Some of the most common broad categories of applications software include word processing, spreadsheets, database management, graphics, desktop publishing, educational, and games.

Word Processing Software **Word processing software**, the most widely used microcomputer software, is designed to make creating, editing, formatting, and printing text easier. The text can consist of correspondence, memos, reports, or even whole books. (This book was written in MS Word 97 running under MS Windows 98.) With a word processor, you can also do some basic typesetting to produce printed documents that rival professionally typeset text. Today's word processors also come with professionally laid-out document *templates*, pre-made document stylesheets, which you can freely use to make your documents look truly professional. Modern word processors offer on-screen formatting capabilities such as font changes, bold text, underlining, and highlighting. With *WYSIWIG* (**W**hat **Y**ou **S**ee **I**s **W**hat **Y**ou **G**et) capabilities, the formatting changes you make are shown on the screen as they will appear when printed out. Word processors usually come equipped with sophisticated spelling checkers, on-line thesauruses, and even grammar-checking functions. Figure 39 shows text and graphics entered into Microsoft Word.

Spreadsheet Software Spreadsheet software uses **spreadsheets** to organize and manipulate data. A spreadsheet is an electronic, on-screen representation of an accountant's columnar pad (like your checkbook register). The display is organized in a format of columns and rows with each column and row intersection forming a box called a *cell*. You can enter one of three types of data into a cell—labels, numbers, or formulas. Once entered, you can perform a myriad of operations on the data, such as calculating, sorting, copying, moving, and formatting. The most valuable function of the electronic spreadsheet is its capability to perform automatic recalculation. When you change a value in the spreadsheet, all values that are dependent on that original value will be automatically recalculated to reflect that change. This ability to change a value and have it automatically reflected throughout the spreadsheet provides the ability to perform *"what-if" analysis*. What if analysis gives us an iterative process where we can try out different values until we get the results we seek. This allows you to propose hypothetical situations and see their projected results. Figure 40 shows quarterly revenues for each business division over the course of a year.

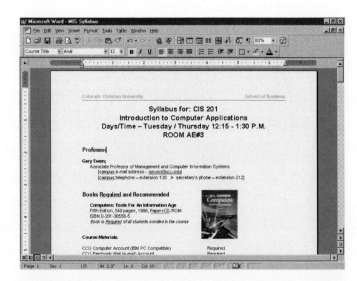

Figure 39 The Microsoft Word 97 word processing application.

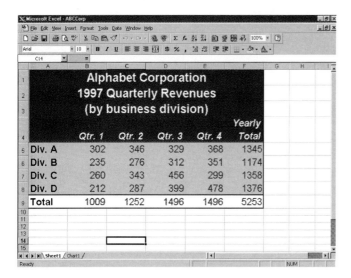

Figure 40 The Microsoft Excel 97 spreadsheet application.

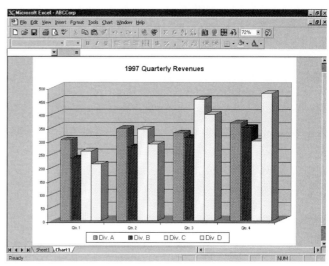

Figure 41 A three-dimensional column chart created from the data in Figure 40.

It has been said that "one picture is worth a thousand words." *Graphs* and charts can show words and numbers in ways that are far more meaningful and more quickly understood. *Charting software,* which usually is included in spreadsheet packages, enables you to visually display data to help in decision making. A stock market analyst could track stock market trends by charting the price of stocks over a period of time. A professor could display the distribution of student grades. The chart in Figure 41 shows quarterly revenues for each business division over the course of a year (the data from Figure 40).

Database Software   A *database management system (DBMS),* such as Claris FileMaker Pro or Microsoft's Access, organizes information that might be related in some way, such as names, addresses, phone numbers, birthdays, and so forth. Databases are good for storing information but they are even better at helping you retrieve information. Database management systems offer an extensive range of sorting, searching, and programming features that enable you to build intricate data management systems. A database, which is a collection of highly structured data, can consist of a warehouse inventory, a mailing list, or even stamp collection data. You can organize your data in your database in one way and later retrieve the same information in a wide variety of ways, depending on your need. DBMS programs allow you to sort, delete, update, and summarize large amounts of data on a computer. The manager of a video store could create a list of videos (a database) and then quickly sort and print the entire list. He or she could then find and edit specific video titles and/or add titles easily. Figure 42 shows a list of customers entered in Claris FileMaker Pro.

Graphics Software   Users can create *graphic* images using painting or drawing software. Both types of software let you create original pictures, but which type of package you use will depend on the specific result that you are looking for, how you want to create the image, and how the image will be stored.

Painting software produces *bitmapped graphics* with which you use a pointing device such as a mouse, a trackball, or a pen on a pressure-sensitive tablet to manipulate individual *pixels* on the screen. The simplest type of bitmapped graphics, called monochrome graphics, merely allows you to turn pixels on and off. One bit stores each pixel's status: l for on and O for off. Pixels that display various shades of gray or different colors store more than one bit of information per pixel. With eight bits of information, a computer can display 256 colors or shades of gray. A photo-quality standard called *true color graphics* can display over l6 million colors but requires 24 bits of information for each pixel on the screen. High-quality bitmapped pictures are notorious for requiring a lot of RAM and large amounts of disk storage space.

In Figure 43, the wallpaper, or background, in Windows 98 is a bitmapped graphic. You can create your own wallpaper similar to this one with a painting program such as Microsoft Paintbrush.

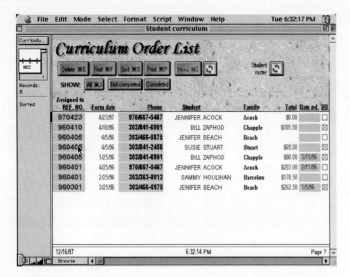

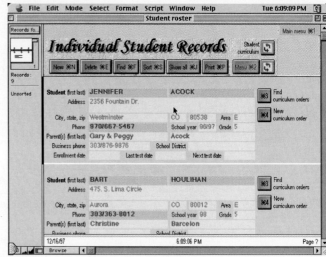

Figure 42 (a) A list of customers in a database management program. (b) Data entry screens for customers in a database program.

Figure 43 A bitmapped screen background image.

Vector graphics, found in drawing software, make fewer demands on both RAM and disk storage space. Data describing the color of each pixel is unnecessary. Vector graphics (also called object-oriented graphics) store all drawn objects as mathematical formulas that represent each object's shape, size, and color. When you load a vector graphic picture, the software performs calculations to determine the pixels the need to be activated to recreate all of the objects. Vector graphic pictures do not look as realistic as bitmapped graphic pictures, but their objects are easier to manipulate.

For example, assume you have drawn an image of the space shuttle in both a bitmapped graphics pro-

gram and a vector graphics program. To rotate the image you would have to erase all the pixels in the bitmapped image and then use a pointing device (mouse or trackball) to activate the new pixels of the rotated image of the space shuttle. Essentially you would erase the old image and draw a brand new one. For a vector graphic image, you would give the command to rotate the image (usually merely by dragging it with the mouse pointer), and the drawing software would perform all the calculations necessary to redraw the rotated image. Because object manipulation is easier using mathematical equations, ***computer-aided design (CAD)*** software packages, which are programs that let architects and engineers create their complex designs, are always based on vector graphics. Figure 44 was drawn in a vector drawing program. Figure 45 shows a drawing made using AutoCAD. Drawing programs like AutoCAD are used to design bridges, buildings, and even cars. SuperPaint is a combination painting and drawing program. The fly in Figure 46 was painted; the rest was drawn.

Communications Software

With a telephone ***modem*** and ***communications software,*** a computer can join the world of ***telecommunications***, which refers to the merger of telephone communications and computers. Communications software, such as Windows' built-in dial-up networking program, controls the flow of data through a modem.

Figure 44 This image was created in a vector graphics program called Corel Draw.

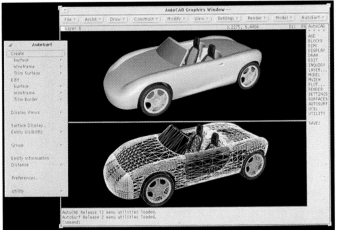

Figure 45 An AutoCad drawing.

Figure 46 A combination of a painted and a drawn image created in SuperPaint.

Computer users who wish to send and receive *electronic mail (e-mail)* will need to invest in an e-mail program. Once your computer is connected to a remote computer or a computer network, programs such as Microsoft Outlook and Lotus cc:Mail enable you to store and sort mail; create and edit mailing lists; search mail by topic, sender, and date; as well as organize mail in topical folders.

Usually a software package is dedicated to one primary application. For example, Microsoft Word is a full-featured word processor with some very rudimentary spreadsheet and database capability built in. Lotus 1-2-3 is a full-featured spreadsheet package with some graphics and database capabilities. *Integrated software* packages are programs that include well-developed components from a variety of application software (usually word processor, spreadsheet, database, and graphics functions). None of these components is as powerful as a stand-alone program ("a jack of many trades and a master of none"). For example, the word processor in Microsoft Works is not as powerful as the dedicated word processor such as Microsoft Word. But for many computer users, programs such as Microsoft Works and ClarisWorks can provide all the functionality they need.

For people who need a wide variety of applications but more power than is available in an integrated software package, there are software suites. A *software suite* is a bundle of full-blown application programs; Microsoft Office Pro comes with Word, Excel, Mail, PowerPoint (a program for making multimedia presentations), and Access (a complete database management system). Lotus Corporation's SmartSuite includes Ami Pro (a high-powered word processor), 1-2-3, Approach (a complete database management system), and several other full-featured programs. Buying a software suite costs much less than buying each program individually.

Many other types of application software are available. *Entertainment software* packages such as games can be found on most computers. *Desktop publishing software* is indispensable for creating professional-looking newsletters, brochures, and reports. Many *educational software* packages are available to teach skills from basic reading and arithmetic to learning a foreign language. Special software is routinely used in the fields of accounting, statistics, geology, and engineering, to name a few.

No matter what application tool you wish to add to your computer system it is important to remember to purchase the version of the software that is appropriate for your computer and operating system—DOS, Windows, or Macintosh. It also important to insure that your computer has the resources required to effectively run the applications software—available space on the hard disk drive, a fast enough processor, and enough RAM. The requirements of the application software should be clearly spelled out on the box in which the new software is packaged.

Programming Languages

Operating systems and application software are written with *programming languages.* Currently, more than 200 programming languages are in use, but only a handful enjoy widespread popularity. They range from low-level languages that work on the computer's level (1s and 0s) to high-level languages that are more like English.

Machine language is a very low-level language that a computer understands. Machine language consists of 0s and 1s. This language is so difficult to learn and use that even most skilled programmers completely avoid it. Assembly language is one step above machine language but it is still complex. Early versions of Word Perfect and Lotus 1-2-3 were written in *assembly language*. Today most programmers prefer to use high-level languages that have a structure much more like that of the English language. Languages such as *C* are used for large projects, such as developing new application software, as well as for smaller projects, such as tracking student grades.

If you do decide to write a program, you can choose from several popular languages. *FORTRAN* (**FOR**mula **TRAN**slator) is still used for many engineering and scientific applications. *COBOL* (**CO**mmon **B**usiness-**O**riented **L**anguage), a relatively old language, is still found in many business environments around the world. *BASIC* (**B**eginners' **A**ll-purpose **S**ymbolic **I**nstruction **C**ode) and *Pascal* (named after the French mathematician Blaise Pascal) are good choices for learning how to program because of their simple approaches. The *C* programming language was originally designed for writing operating systems, but its high degree of sophistication has made it a popular language for developing new application software at companies such as Lotus, Microsoft, and Borland. *Visual Basic* and *Visual C++* are relatively new object-oriented programming languages that were specially designed to develop applications for GUI environments. *Java* and *Eiffel* are newer programming languages that are designed to develop applications for GUI environments that run over the Internet.

Today average users usually do not need to write programs to solve problems. Packaged programs such as Claris FileMaker Pro, Corel Draw, Lotus 1-2-3, and Microsoft Word can solve many problems that in the past required extensive programming.

Types of Computers

Computers vary from small, single-user machines that fit into the palm of your hand to large, powerful, multi-user computers that can process billions of instructions per second.

Supercomputers, Mainframes, and Minicomputers

The National Center for Atmospheric Research (NCAR) in Boulder, Colorado provides a superb infrastructure to advance human understanding of the Earth's climate systems. NCAR house two supercomputers (the most powerful computing machines in the world). Together, these *supercomputers* can process more than two billion *floating point operations (FLOPS) per second.* All of this massive computing power does carry a hefty price tag and supercomputers can cost up to $30 million or more. Because of the price, only large organizations with tremendous data-manipulation requirements procure supercomputers. Government agencies doing weather forecasting or weapons research are typical supercomputer customers.

Before the supercomputer, the *mainframe* computer was the processing heavyweight champion. IBM became a leading multinational corporation selling mainframes to medium-sized and large organizations such as insurance companies, banks, and airlines.

In 1952, after counting just five percent of the vote, UNIVAC I mainframe computer (see Figure 47) correctly predicted that Dwight D. Eisenhower would win the presidential election. And yet today's microcomputers are unbelievably faster, smaller, and much easier to use.

Airline reservation systems are typical of mainframe applications. In this case, a system called *timesharing* enables multiple ticket agents (in airports and reservation centers all over the world) to be linked simultaneously with one mainframe. Each ticket agent has his or her own terminal, a keyboard and screen, but the CPU in the mainframe computer is shared. Timesharing software enables the CPU to switch its attention from one terminal to another to perform a small part of each ticket agent's task in a short, specified period. The CPU processes information so quickly that each agent seems to have the mainframe's undivided attention. The same process

Figure 47 The UNIVAC I.

occurs when bank tellers access a central computer or when you withdraw money from an automatic teller machine (ATM), a commonly used terminal. You may not realize it, but when you use an ATM, you are sharing CPU time with many other users.

Since they were developed in the 1940s, and until minicomputers arrived in the 1960s, mainframes were the only computers available. *Minicomputers*, which are essentially scaled-down mainframes, were a major development because they delivered timesharing capabilities at a much lower price. Smaller organizations, such as retail businesses, colleges, and state and city agencies, could afford minicomputers. Today, many colleges and universities use minicomputers to run their registration systems. Course information is entered into terminals (at some universities, a touch-tone telephone can serve as a terminal) connected to a minicomputer.

Microcomputers and Workstations

The distinctions among mainframes, minicomputers, and smaller computers are blurring with each passing day. Today's PCs are many times more powerful than mainframes or minicomputers of only ten years ago. Some top-of-the-line PC models can compete with current minicomputers in processing power, and in the near future you could very likely have the power of a mainframe on your desk. Indeed, many technology industry analysts predict that you will have supercomputer power in your personal computer in as little as ten years (see the section titled "What's in Store for Tomorrow" near the end of the book).

Personal computers, also known as **microcomputers,** first appeared in the mid-1970s in a ready-to-assemble kit (see Figure 48). If you had $400 or so, very good technical skills, and a few weeks on your hands, you could build an MITS Altair 8800 computer that lacked a keyboard and screen (input was handled with switches; output, with a series of small lights). To make your computing experience even more challenging, you were *required* to write your own software because application software like WordPerfect, Microsoft Word, and Lotus 1-2-3 did not exist. Today you can find an Altair 8800 displayed in the Boston Computer Museum.

Microcomputers are now found almost everywhere. Many organizations have switched their employees from dumb terminals (without processors) hooked to mainframes and minicomputers to microcomputers connected via a network. Your college computer lab is probably filled with microcomputers made by Apple, IBM, Hewlett-Packard, Dell, AST, Compaq, or some other computer company. Not all microcomputers sit on top of a desk. Figure 49 shows the Power Macintosh computer, which has a system box called a **mini-tower** that is designed to stand under or next to a table or desk.

Between the world of microcomputers and minicomputers is a single-user computer, called a workstation, that approaches the power of a mainframe. Typically used by designers, workstations have large screens and abundant processing muscle to handle the drawings of engineers, architects, and graphic designers. The SUN workstation shown in Figure 50 has a large screen that can display more

Figure 48 The Altair 8800 was the first microcomputer and was very difficult to use.

Figure 49 The PowerMac microcomputer.

Figure 50 A SUN workstation.

than 16.7 million colors. The term workstation can be used to describe either any computer at which you do your work in a network or a powerful single-user computer used by someone involved in sophisticated design.

Portable Computers

Several years after the first microcomputers appeared, someone decided this great business tool should be portable. Computer makers such as Compaq and Osborne placed a CPU, a shrunken (5-inch) CRT, a small detachable keyboard, a floppy disk drive, and a few other goodies into a suitcase-size package with a handle on top. Weighing 25 pounds or more, these systems could be lugged around if necessary, but they hardly compare to today's truly portable computers.

Today you can get a *notebook* computer that, at seven pounds or less, is truly portable. Almost everything you can find in a full-size desktop microcomputer is now available in a notebook computer: fast Pentium or PowerPC CPUs, hard disk drives of up to 5 GB or more, fax/modems, floppy disk drives, CD-ROMs, pointing devices, and so on. The only possible drawback of notebooks is their LCDs, which lag behind CRTs in size, brightness, and speed.

The Sony VAIO shown in Figure 51 is a very powerful computer in a handy notebook configuration. It is equipped with a 233 MHz Intel® Pentium® processor with MMX technology, 32 MB of RAM, and a superior 12.1" XGA Active Matrix LCD display. It also features a 2.1 GB hard disk drive, an integral 33.6 kbps modem with 14.4 kbps fax capability, and built-in stereo speakers. In addition, the computer has a 14x CD-ROM drive as well as a floppy disk drive and a built-in digital touchpad pointing device and microphone. The two PCMCIA slots can accept any type of industry standard credit card devices (such as network interface cards, cellular modems, etc.), and battery life can exceed five hours of continuous use—all at less than six pounds!

Some portable computers are getting even smaller. More computing power is being built into *sub-notebook* and *palmtop* configurations all the time, as is illustrated in Figure 52, which shows a Toshiba Libretto sub-notebook computer. Although not as feature rich as the Sony Notebook computer, the Libretto 70CT combines the power of Windows 95, a 1.5 GB hard disk drive, 16 MB of high-speed EDO DRAM, and an Intel 120 MHz Pentium® processor with MMX technology for enhanced audio and video performance. It also features a bright 6.1" TFT active matrix color display with 640 × 480 resolution for crisp and clear definition. Weighing in at just 1.88 pounds and 8.3" × 4.5" × 1.4" in size, the Libretto 70CT offers portability and functionality that goes far beyond most handheld PCs.

Because manufacturers are building computers that are so small, notebook computer manufacturers have devised clever methods for adding extra equipment and for pointing to objects on the screen. Most notebooks have **P**ersonal **C**omputer **M**emory **C**ard **I**nternational **A**ssociation *(PCMCIA)* slots that accept special credit card-size devices, such as a modem, a network interface card, or extra RAM. Figure 53 shows a PCMCIA slot and card.

Most people using a portable computer don't have the desk space to use a mouse. *Trackballs* are typically found in front of the keyboard on many notebook computers. Some companies (like IBM and Toshiba) have placed their pointing devices in the middle of the keyboard as shown in Figure 54.

Figure 51 The Sony VAIO notebook computer.

Figure 53 PCMCIA cards can be easily inserted and removed, allowing the user to quickly and easily add functional components to the computer system.

Figure 52 A Toshiba Libretto sub-notebook computer.

Figure 54 The TrackPoint II found on IBM notebook computers.

These devices, which look and feel like an eraser at the tip of a pencil, allow the computer user to keep his or her hands on the keyboard while moving the pointer on the screen. Many notebook computers have a touch-sensitive touchpad located just below the keyboard. The pointer on the screen moves in the same direction as the user's finger on the touchpad.

Palmtop computers can be held in one hand easily. 3-COM's PalmPilot and IBM's WorkPad PC (see Figure 55) are so small that they have no disk drives but do have several applications built in on ROM chips. Palmtop computers can even accept input entered by a small pen-like stylus that can read your writing. After entering data, you can connect these tiny computers to your larger desktop or notebook computer via a "synchronization cradle" in order to transfer data.

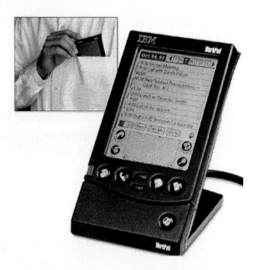

Figure 55 The light 6-ounce palmtop computer gives you instant access and update capability for your Address Book, Date Book, and To Do Lists as well as convenient e-mail or Internet connectivity. Only 4.7" tall and 3.2" wide, these new palmtop computers are truly carry-anywhere "pocket" PC companions.

Multimedia

Millions of computer users have taken the multimedia plunge. *Multimedia* involves interactively using animation, photos, video, and sound on a computer. You need special equipment, databases, and software to join this exciting world.

Almost any computer user interested in interactive computing will be interested in multimedia. In addition to *reading* about Martin Luther King, Jr., on the computer screen, you can also see and hear him. Instead of deciphering complex repair manuals, you can use a multimedia system to help you fix machinery using interactive animations, just as the Air Force and Otis Elevator currently do.

Hardware for Interactive Computing

The bare essentials for a multimedia computer are a CD-ROM drive, a sound card, speakers, and a microphone. All multimedia hardware fits into the five hardware categories: a CD-ROM drive is secondary storage, a sound card and speakers are output, and a microphone is input. Figure 56 shows an Apple Macintosh computer, which comes with all the standard multimedia devices, including a CD-ROM drive, a sound card, and speakers.

A picture may well be worth a thousand words, but it also requires thousands (or even millions) of

Figure 56 A multimedia computer.

bytes of disk storage. Video clips and sound can take up even more space. Placing an entire interactive encyclopedia on a CD-ROM is possible only because CD-ROMs can store more than half a billion bytes of information.

The Microsoft Encarta 98 CD-ROM uses audio, video, maps, charts, graphs, still photos, and a wealth of data to bring the Funk and Wagnall's encyclopedia to life. Figure 57 shows a screen from Microsoft Encarta, which is the best selling encyclopedia of all time (computerized or bound). This CD-ROM includes more than 30,000 authoritative articles—4,000 new and updated for 1998—more than 2,500 links to the Internet, and more than 300,000 links to related topics. Encarta 98 includes over 7,000 photos and illustrations, eight hours of sound, and hundreds of animations and video clips.

Simple video clips found on CD-ROM encyclopedias do not require special equipment. However, if you plan to capture and replay your own video images, you'll need a video camera, a video capture card, and an accelerated display adapter for your video screen (monitor). A video capture card can digitize video sequences from virtually any video source: television set, VCR, DVD, or video camera (camcorder). Keep in mind that video recordings take up an incredible amount of storage space and require very fast processors and a lot of RAM. There are several methods of decreasing the storage requirements of video, including storing fewer frames per second (video cameras normally capture 30 frames per second), replaying the recording in a smaller window on the display screen (smaller images require less disk space), and compressing the video file. In order to recreate the original video data, the file would then be decompressed. Sophisticated algorithms are used to compress and decompress files.

The CPU in a typical computer usually handles all of the video, but for multimedia computers it is wise to add an ***accelerated video adapter card***. Accelerated video adapter cards have an extra processor that frees the CPU to do other things, such as performing calculations and overseeing system resources. Although these adapter cards are not required for multimedia, using them can dramatically improve the manipulation of video images.

There are several ways to work with photographs on a multimedia computer. Most CD-ROM drives are compatible with Kodak's Photo CD system (see Figure 58). You can place a roll of pictures on a CD by having the roll of film developed at a photo store

(a)

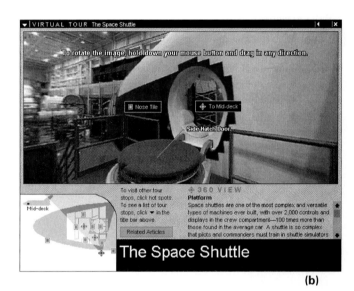

(b)

Figure 57 (a) An interactive multimedia article on the space shuttle. The small window is actually an audio/video sequence showing a shuttle launch. (b) An interactive, "virtual tour" of the space shuttle.

equipped to handle photo CDs. Up to 100 images—about four 24-exposure rolls of film—can be placed on one Photo CD. The photos can then be displayed on the computer screen and can be digitally manipulated to change how they appear.

Some companies such as Corel sell Photo CDs filled with high-quality pictures taken by professional photographers. Each CD comes with 100 related photos on topics such as lighthouses, flowers, mountains, cowboys, or windsurfing. Corel's Photo CD collection now numbers in the hundreds of CDs.

Figure 58 A Kodak Photo CD.

Photos can be input to the computer via a digital-scanning device as well. A *scanner* is capable of "reading" a printed page or image (similar to a copy machine), translating the visual representation of that image into digital pulses (1s and 0s), and then inputting the digital data to the computer system for processing, storage, and eventual output. Low-cost handheld scanners are available for simple home use. Sheetfed scanners are available for scanning both images and text on individual sheets of paper and flatbed scanners are available for scanning images from bound volumes.

You can also place photos directly into the computer with a *digital camera*. Small in size, digital cameras take very high quality digital photos. Digital cameras are having a profound affect on the art of photography. They work by capturing images on a computer chip instead of light sensitive film and then temporarily storing each image in RAM. So without having to submit your valuable pictures for processing at a processing plant, you can display, store, edit, and print your images from your computer. Many digital cameras are capable of storing similar numbers of photographs before you must download them to your computer via an interface cable. The standard SVGA display screen on most computers can adequately handle most multimedia images. "Developing" of the image takes only seconds, and many digital cameras are equipped with small color LCD screens so that you can preview images and delete any unsatisfactory ones.

Once your photos are input into your computer, you may wish to edit or resize them with *image editing software*. Image editing software will also allow you to modify and enhance the photograph

by changing colors, contrast, brightness, size, and shape. You can use image editing software to "doctor" photographs, adding or removing elements from the picture or even combining multiple photos into one final composite picture.

Like most issues regarding the computer, there are qualitative differences in scanners and digital cameras. The primary goal should be to get the highest resolution (the most dots) that you can afford. Some scanners and digital cameras are capable of capturing *VGA* quality images (640×480) while others have *SVGA* capabilities (800×600 or even higher). Obviously, the higher the quality of the images (resolution) the larger the storage space that will be required and the more RAM required to digitally manipulate the image. If still photos just won't do the trick, digital video cameras are also available. With digital video camera and video capture interface boards you can input full-motion video sequences, complete with sound, into your computer for editing and playback. Figure 59 shows a small, lightweight, inexpensive digital video camera.

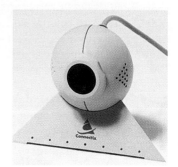

Figure 59 Connected to the computer by an interface cable, this video camera can take either still or motion picture images of you and digitize them so that they can be processed by the computer.

A *sound card* is a circuit board that plugs into the main system board in a computer and provides the ability to generate speech and music through speakers that plug directly into the card. Most sound cards also offer the opportunity of plugging in a microphone to record speech or brief sound clips. In the mid-1980s the first 8-bit sound cards were manufactured for PCs. The 8-bit feature simply refers to the rate at which the card processes data. The more bits that can be processed, the better the performance in terms of sound quality. The sound "resolution," or sampling rate, of these early cards was either 11 or 22 *kilohertz (kHz)*; the higher sampling rates resulted in higher quality sound. Today's sound cards are typically 16- or 32-bit sound cards and some are available for a full "3-D" quality sound experience. Remember that as sound card technology has developed so has the storage requirements for sound. To save one minute of recorded 8-bit sound at 11 kHz requires approximately 330 KB of storage space. Double the **sampling rate** to 22 kHz and the storage requirement will double to 660 KB of storage space. One minute of recorded 16-bit, 44 kHz sound requires 10 MB of storage space. Many sound cards have a Multimedia PC Rating Council (MPC) rating. The MPC develops minimum standards for multimedia hardware and software known as MPC1, MPC2, and MPC3 (with MPC3 being the best quality).

Many sound cards include a **musical instrument digital interface (MIDI)** hookup for connecting musical instruments directly to the computer, such as a special MIDI keyboard or MIDI guitar. MIDI is a music notation system that enables electronic instruments and computers to communicate with each other. Through MIDI you can record on a computer the exact keystrokes from a MIDI keyboard and then play back the music using a sound card. You can also write music by inputting the music into the computer (see Figure 60) and then editing the digital notes until you have the precise composition of music that you desire. Another

possibility is buying prerecorded MIDI music to edit and playback through your sound card.

Sound cards have evolved to a standard called **wavetable-synthesis**, which uses **digital signal processors (DSP)** to digitally sample actual sounds from real instruments or voices. These digitally sampled sounds result in true high quality reproduction of musical instruments during playback.

Figure 60 A MIDI system allows computers to be interfaced with electronic musical instruments.

Applying Multimedia

Most people have been exposed to multimedia through flashy video games or other types of home entertainment. True multimedia is much more. Many schools, from the primary level through universities, are using multimedia to teach topics such

as foreign languages and math. The U.S. Navy and companies such as Otis Elevator use multimedia systems to train maintenance and repair workers. United Airlines uses multimedia simulators to train pilots.

When you are ready to move beyond using prepackaged multimedia applications and develop your own, you will need a **multimedia authoring tool**. Multimedia authoring tools are used to create interactive presentations. You can create sales presentations, training systems, or even games. Authoring packages range from easy-to-use presentation management programs to high-powered professional systems.

Presentation management software, such as Microsoft PowerPoint and Lotus Freelance, allows you to automate multimedia presentations. Typically, computerized presentations are based on "slides," which are similar to transparencies or photographic slides but are actually on-screen digital media. You create one slide after another on the screen, incorporating text, photos, graphics, drawings, animations, video sequences, and so on. During a presentation, the slides are shown in sequence. The slide in Figure 61 was created in Microsoft PowerPoint.

Full-featured authoring tools, such as MacroMedia Director, have powerful animation and video manipulation features, but also significant learning curves and hefty price tags. However, if you dedicate a lot of time and effort into learning one of these programs, you can end up with very professional

Figure 61 A slide presentation created in MS PowerPoint 97.

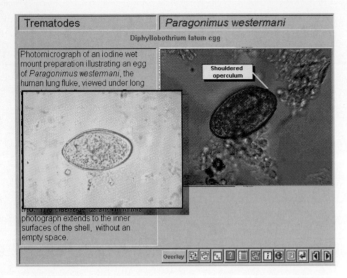

| Trematodes | *Paragonimus westermani* |

Diphyllobothrium latum egg

Photomicrograph of an iodine wet mount preparation illustrating an egg of *Paragonimus westermani*, the human lung fluke, viewed under long

Shouldered operculum

photograph extends to the inner surfaces of the shell, without an empty space.

Overlay

Figure 62 A sample screen from Germware Parasitology.

interactive multimedia presentations and training systems. Instructional Design Consultants, Inc. developed the multimedia title *GermWare Parasitology* shown in Figure 62. This comprehensive multimedia learning system introduces medical technology students to the fundamentals of parasitology. Germware integrates text, graphics, and video into four main lessons that last a total of sixteen hours. The course was developed using Multimedia ToolBook by the Asymetrix Corporation, a full-featured multimedia authoring system.

Computer Networking

A ***network*** is an interconnected collection of computers that enables the sharing of hardware, software, and data. Once the local computer is connected, you become a network user—a person who has access to the resources available on the network. Your ability to communicate with others creates new ways of working together that, without a network, would be difficult or impossible.

Network Hardware

Networks are generally classified by size: networks serving a local area and networks serving a wide area. A ***local area network (LAN)***, which is a network of small computers, connects a small business or a department within a large organization and is usually located in one building or in buildings that are close to each other. The computer where a person works, called a workstation (the term client is also used), typically is a microcomputer. A ***server***, which is a computer that "serves" the network, is typically a powerful microcomputer or sometimes a minicomputer.

A ***wide area network (WAN)*** connects computers across a city, state, or even the entire planet. WANs consist of almost any size computer and often include LANs that are connected together. If you have a computer with a modem at home, chances are that you can dial in to a computer network at school and then access any WAN to which your school is attached. A set of electronic signals (such as a document) could travel through a LAN on a copper cable and then be beamed from a local microwave tower. The signal could then bounce off a satellite to its destination computer attached to a LAN on the other side of the world, as shown in Figure 63.

There are two ways to connect computers: by cables and via wireless systems. LANs typically use cables but ***wireless networks*** are growing in popularity. Figure 64 shows an unshielded twisted-pair wire similar to telephone wire and relatively inexpensive. The coaxial cable in Figure 65 (a close cousin to the coaxial cable that connects a TV to cable TV systems) is also very popular for LANs. A thin glass fiber called fiber optic cabling carries signals as pulses of light. No cable transmits signals faster than fiber optic cable. Which cable is used depends on the desired speed, the budget, and which communications standards are being followed. Fiber optic cabling is displayed in Figure 66.

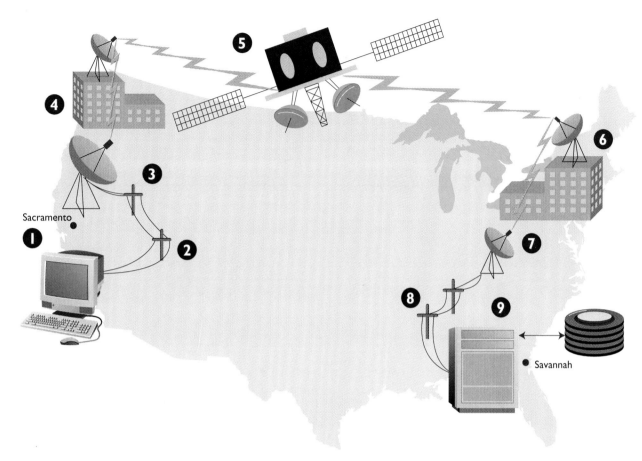

Figure 63 A wide variety of communication links can be combined to create a wide area network (WAN).

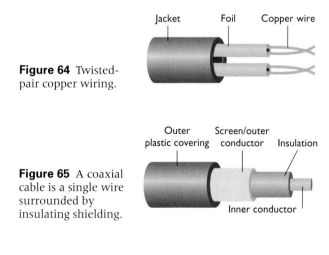

Figure 64 Twisted-pair copper wiring.

Figure 65 A coaxial cable is a single wire surrounded by insulating shielding.

Figure 66 Fiber optic cables consist of hair-thin fibers of glass that can carry video, voice, and data signals.

The most popular communications standard for transporting information throughout a LAN is called *Ethernet*. One type of Ethernet network consists of a long *coaxial cable*, called a *backbone*, that winds through the rooms of a building. As shown in Figure 67, each computer connects to the coaxial backbone, often referred to as a bus configuration, through a T-connector attached to a network interface card in the computer (see Figure 68). This standard configuration defines *data transmission speeds* of up to 10 Mbps (megabits per second) and is called a 10Base2 network. Setting up a 10Base2 network is relatively simple and inexpensive. However, these networks are not as robust and stable as other network configurations. Figure 69 shows another type of Ethernet network configuration. In this layout, computers are typically connected via unshielded twisted-pair wire to a *hub*, which is a device that physically connects two or more cables together. A hub provides a central location from which network cables spread out and attach to computers. This type of network is often

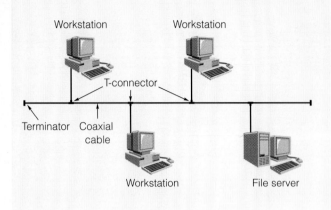

Figure 67 A typical Bus topology network.

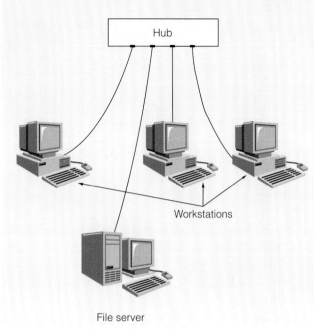

Figure 69 A computer network using a centralized hub.

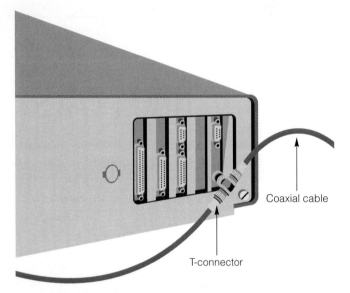

Figure 68 The T-connector is attached to the network interface card at the back of the computer.

referred to as a 10BaseT network. Although a 10BaseT is more expensive to install, it is more stable than a 10Base2 network and can reach data transmission speeds from 10 Mbps to 100 Mbps.

In any Ethernet network, each attached computer is "listening" to the cable, waiting for a break in the network traffic before sending out any data. If two computers try to send data at precisely the same fraction of a second, a *data collision* occurs. After a data collision is detected, each computer will wait a preset amount of time before attempting to retransmit the data. This transmission strategy is called *carrier sense multiple access with collision detect (CSMA/CD).*

Sharing Software and Data

Once a network is physically connected with network interface cards, cables, hubs, servers, and so forth, you are almost ready to start sharing network resources. The *network operating system (NOS)* must be loaded onto the server and all *client* computers in order to supervise the operations of the network. The most popular network operating systems on networks today are Microsoft Corporations Windows NT and Novell Corporation's NetWare. The main part of the operating system will be located on the network file server while a smaller network software component called a *client* will be loaded on each user computer that is to be attached to the network. Each local networked computer (called a *network node*) will also be running a separate operating system in addition to the network client software. Microsoft Windows NT network servers can be accessed by nodes running Novell, Windows, MacOS, Windows 95, Windows 98, and Windows NT operating systems.

The network and local operating systems work hand in hand behind the scenes to ensure that everything runs smoothly. For example, if you are sitting at a network node computer and you double click on an icon to load an application software package from the file server, the local operating system will hand off this command to the network operating system. The network operating system will then open the requested software from the file server and send the program down the network cables to the local workstation. At that point, the local operating system makes sure that the application software is started successfully. If there are any problems, the two operating systems (local and network) will work together to resolve the issue. Of course, all of this works behind the scenes and is very transparent to the end user.

The main purpose of local area networks is to reduce costs, minimize effort, and promote collaboration among users. Instead of having to purchase one copy of application software for *each* computer, one copy can be loaded onto the central server and then shared by all workstations on the network. A special network version of the application software, called a *site license,* must be obtained and software licenses must be purchased for each computer on the network that will be using the software. But this is usually much less expensive than buying multiple copies of software. For example, instead of buying a printer for each computer, you can buy one or two higher quality printers that everyone can share over the network.

Communicating and Collaborating

In addition to accessing software or data from a file server, network users can communicate with each other. *E-mail* is an important network application. An e-mail server program is loaded onto the file server and client e-mail software (compatible with the server e-mail software) is loaded onto each local network workstation. You can use e-mail programs such as Microsoft Mail, MS Outlook (see Figure 70), Eudora, Lotus cc:Mail, or ClarisMail to send messages to another user's mailbox. In this sense, the term mailbox refers to a small storage area on the file server's hard disk. When the recipient logs into the network and checks his or her mailbox, your message will be there. Besides saving paper, e-mail has numerous other advantages over regular mail. E-mail can be easily forwarded to another user, sent to multiple users simultaneously, and sorted and saved in categories by subject, date, sender, and so forth. In addition, almost instantaneously mail can be sent anywhere in the world and the sender can check to see whether the recipient has read the mail.

FYI   One of the problems with digital communication in the form of e-mail is that it can often come across as impersonal. Face-to-face communication is multifaceted because you can see a person's body language, gestures, and facial expressions while hearing the inflections in their voice.

E-mail doesn't afford the ability for such rich communication. A small but important technique used to express emotions within the limits of e-mail is the use of emoticons, a few of which follow. If you tilt your head to the left and look at the emoticon, you'll see that each one represents a little facial expression.

:-D	Big smile	>:-<	Mad
:-/	Skeptical	:'-(	Crying
:-*	Oops	:-o	Surprised
:-(	Frowning	:->	Sarcastic
:-&	Tongue tied	;-)	Winking
:-@	Screaming	:-O	Uh Oh
:-S	Incoherent	:-)	Smile
:'->	Happy and crying		

Remember that e-mail can be misunderstood easily because it lacks the many and varied "channels" of communication that we've come to take for granted in face-to-face communication. Be very careful how you express yourself through e-mail.

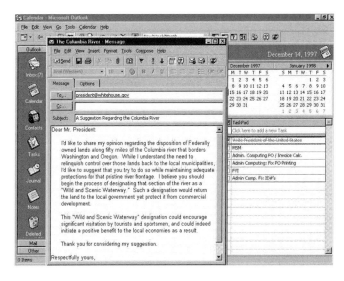

Figure 70 Microsoft Outlook e-mail client.

Networks have also enabled workers to use technology to bring people and their ideas together despite geographic barriers. While e-mail can certainly assist in this goal, now network computers are capable of videoconferencing as well. Videoconferencing can include small video cameras mounted on computer displays that send live pictures so that two or more workers can communicate right from their workstations. Some videoconferencing systems consist of large screen displays and multiple cameras in order to facilitate large group collaboration.

Sharing data is another tremendous advantage of network computing. Networks and *groupware* are enabling *workgroup* computing solutions, a kind of software application that is specifically designed to encourage groups of people to work collaboratively on projects. *Electronic data interchange (EDI)* is also enabled through network computing. EDI is a series of formats that allow businesses to transmit electronically invoices, purchase orders, and such. Using *electronic fund transfers (EFTs),* businesses and individuals can pay for goods and services by having funds transferred from one account to another electronically. Another outcome of network computing is the growing practice of *telecommuting*, using computers and communications technology to replace the commute from home to work and accomplish daily work-related tasks from home.

Traveling on the Information Highway

Imagine sitting at a computer at home and dialing a local telephone number to access another computer that has late-breaking news, stock market quotes, access to your bank account, games, catalogs for shopping, magazines, an encyclopedia, and the ability to make travel arrangements for you. Would you pay to access such a computer? *Commercial information services* such as America Online offer all of these services and much more for a small monthly fee.

What if you could log on to a workstation in a network that was connected to another network, which was connected to yet another network, which was connected to a giant web of networks that spanned the entire planet? What kind of people might you find out there to whom you could communicate? What kind of databases might be available? What kind of information resources could you find? Such a giant network does indeed exist—it's called the *Internet*.

Commercial Information Services

A large number of information systems offer their services and resources to the public. You must pay to use many of them but some may be free. For example, if you want to look up late-breaking news or make an airline reservation, you could sign up with an online information service provider like CompuServe, Prodigy, America Online, or the Microsoft Network. Figure 71 is a sample of America Online screens that show some of the broad information categories that are available. You can also send e-mail to anyone else in the world who has an e-mail account. If you want to exchange ideas and information with others, you can use one of these commercial services to "connect" computer users who might have similar interests.

To connect to an online information provider, all you have to do is load the software (provided free by the service provider) and answer a few questions about who you are and how you intend to pay (usually by credit card). Through your online service provider you can access news, weather, e-mail, shopping, educational materials and programs, research databases, financial information, special interest group forums, and much more. America Online (AOL) has become the most popular online

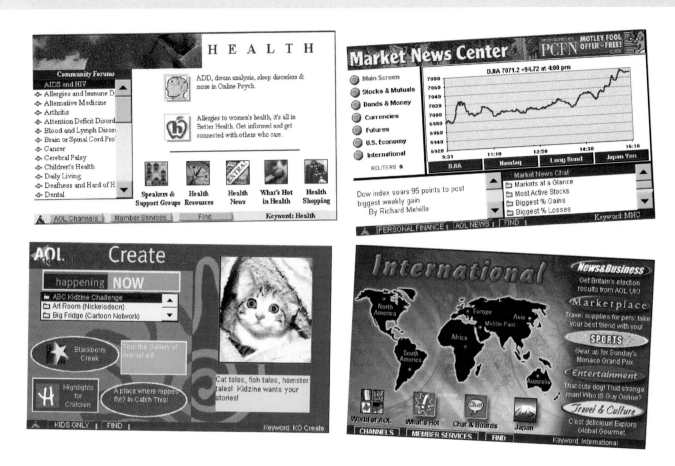

Figure 71 Online service providers like America Online provide a wide array of information resources.

information service provider with its easy-to-use graphical user interface. Online service providers are offering more and more features than ever before. The information accessible from online services is proprietary in nature and runs the spectrum from how to train your dog to actual online celebrity appearances. Online service providers also offer access to the Internet, although a user primarily interested in the Internet may do well by signing up for only Internet service via an *Internet service provider (ISP)*.

The Internet

From your dorm room, your den, or your college classroom, chances are good that you can dial a local telephone number and connect with the biggest computer network in the world. It's completely legal. It may even be free. It's the Internet!

The groundwork for the information superhighway has been laid through the Internet, a global net-

work of networks, large and small, that connects universities, government agencies, military sites, public organizations, and private companies. The Internet originated in the late 1960s as the *ARPAnet*, an experimental network for the Advanced Research Projects Agency (ARPA) which was a subset of the Department of Defense. The network was designed to withstand a nuclear war by virtue of its decentralized nature. No single point of failure anywhere on the network could bring down the entire network. If a segment of the network malfunctioned or was destroyed, the data on the network would simply select a different route to arrive at its intended destination.

To send a message on this network of networks, a computer placed data into an electronic envelope called the *Internet protocol (IP)* packet. Over the years, many other networks evolved using the same IP communications standard. One of the networks called the NSFnet, run by the National Science Foundation (NSF), connected five supercomputing centers across the United States. The NSF plan was to connect major universities to these supercomputer sites to facilitate scholarly research. The NSFnet eventually replaced ARPAnet as the primary backbone of what was to later become the Internet.

Today, most colleges and universities (and many high schools and elementary schools) are connected to the Internet. Many colleges and universities offer Internet accounts to their students. Many large corporations have had Internet connections for years, and more and more small companies are getting connected all the time. Even home computer users can connect to the Internet by paying a monthly fee to an Internet service provider (ISP), a company that helps individuals get on the Internet and use the Internet's vast services. Whether you connect to the Internet through an ISP or through an online service provider, you will be joining tens of millions of other current users, and millions more are joining every year. When you connect to the Internet, your computer becomes an extension of what seems like a single giant computer—a computer with branches all over the world. Welcome to the fastest growing communication medium on earth!

The Internet is similar to a wide area network (WAN), but it is structured very differently. A WAN is a single network with a cohesive structure and chances are only one group of people is responsible for maintaining the whole thing. The Internet consists of thousands of loosely connected networks and no single group of people is responsible for it. However, there are some rules (called *protocols*) and systems architectures to which everyone must adhere.

The Internet is structured such that each network on the Internet is independent, but each network communicates with the Internet using the same networking language (Internet protocol) called IP. This agreed upon protocol is similar to when, years ago, railroad owners agreed upon a standard railroad gauge so that they could link one railroad with another.

The Internet is a cooperative society that forms a "virtual" community covering the entire globe. Think of the Internet as a giant computer "co-op." The Internet is the gateway to *cyberspace*, the "virtual universe" of ideas and information we enter whenever we use a computer, except this virtual universe is made up of bits, not atoms. The Internet allows you to "travel" through global cyberspace using your computer.

FYI The Internet is organized into six major groups, or domains:

- .com Commercial organizations
- .edu Educational institutions
- .gov Government sites
- .mil Military sites
- .net Major network support centers
- .org Other organizations such as nonprofits

Each country on the Internet (currently there are more than 130 of them) has a domain. Here are some examples:

- .au Australia
- .ch China
- .ca Canada
- .uk United Kingdom
- .jp Japan
- .us United States (although the .us is assumed if you don't designate it)

One common use of the Internet is to send and receive e-mail. If you have an account, you can send a message to another user by using the Internet's *Domain Naming System (DNS)*, a hierarchical system that uses domains, sub-domains, and host computer names to narrow down the location of a computer on the Internet. A computer connected to the Internet could have many users, each with a name that uniquely identifies that particular user. Thus, your organization might have a LAN—or perhaps even a WAN—and your network administrator might allow access from the LAN/WAN to the Internet. Remember that your organization is responsible for its part of the LAN/WAN and somewhat responsible for its connection to the Internet, but it is not responsible for anything else on the Internet.

Each network connects to the Internet through a device called a *router*. The main purpose of the router with regard to the Internet is to keep information on the Internet flowing to its intended destination. When data arrives at the router, the router checks to see whether that data is addressed to a computer within that router's domain. If not, the router will simply send the data along the best possible route to another router. If the data is intended for a computer within that router's domain, the router delivers it to the appropriate

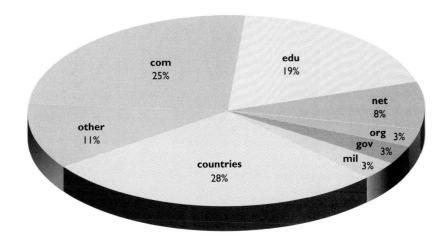

Figure 72 This pie chart shows the approximate relative sizes of the top-level Internet domain names.

subordinate router or to the appropriate file server or end-user computer.

Unlike a railroad, there is really no way to define where the Internet is physically located. The hardware for the Internet consists of the computers attached to the network and all of the cables and routers between them. Therefore, in one sense, the Internet is at every computer and router on every network and all of the telephone cables and all the satellite parts of our global telecommunications system—and those "parts" come and go. Because the Internet is a network of networks, no one owns the whole thing. Each company, university, government, or organization owns its part of the network. Different companies and government agencies own the "glue" (hardware and software) that holds the various parts together, but they do not own the information that passes though the Internet.

So who controls the Internet? Because of its planned lack of structure, when a small segment of the Internet fails, the owner of that section fixes the problem while network traffic goes around it. Anyone can make any type of information available on the Internet, even information that you do not like or to which you may not want to be exposed. There is no one centralized place to complain about something on the Internet as each site on the Internet is responsible for its own content.

So how does the message get through to the correct address? The answer lies in the definition of the Internet as a network of networks. All a computer on the Internet needs to know to send a message

(or data) to another computer on the Internet is the address of the destination computer. For example, the *address* of the destination computer might be **38.251.91.0**. This address could be viewed as the **0** computer on network **91**, which is on the larger network numbered **251**, which in turn resides on the largest network number **38**. These numeric addresses are difficult for people to remember, so Internet users typically specify the entities of Internet hosts as "names" such as **whitehouse.gov** or **microsoft.com** or **ccu.edu**. The names are called *uniform resource locators (URLs)*. Two types of entities have Internet addresses: computers and people. Computers on the Internet have addresses that make it easy for you to specify which computer you wish to access. People who have accounts on a particular computer have an address that is made up of their user account name and the name of the computer. The domain naming system starts with some standard domains that appear on the far right of a computer's name. Figure 72 illustrates how the DNS is divided up among Internet users.

A computer's name (or URL) has at least two levels of domain, and each level is separated by a period. To the left of the top-level domain is another name and possibly more than one name. In the domain naming system, each level on the left is a subset of the domain on the right. For example, in the name **luke.ccu.edu**, **luke** is a sub-domain of **ccu**, which in turn is a sub-domain of **edu**. So you might want to read this address somewhat backwards: you are navigating within the **edu** domain to a specific university computer. The name of the university com-

```
URL:
http://www.intel.com/homecomputing/index.htm
```
Protocol   ISP address   Path, directory,
             (domain)   file name

Figure 73 Deconstructing a URL: The uniform resource locator represents a unique address of an Internet resource. This example represents the web address for the host computer at the Intel Corporation and specifically a file called *index.htm,* which is located within the home computing directory on that host computer.

puter is **ccu** (for Colorado Christian University) and the specific computer at CCU is called **luke**. Once on Luke, various directories would be further delineated by their appropriate directory name. Figure 73 illustrates a dissected Internet address called a Uniform Resource Locator (URL).

A person's address is simply the name of his or her account on the computer, followed by an "at" symbol (@), followed by the name of the computer on which the account is registered. For example, my e-mail address is **gewen@ccu.edu**. This represents the first letter of my first name, followed by my last name, followed by the @ symbol, followed by the university domain ccu.edu. So if I wanted to send the President of the United States an e-mail message, I would send it from **gewen@ccu.edu** to **president @whitehouse.gov**. How does this message physically travel from Gary Ewen to the president? I could sit at any computer on any of CCU's campus sites and log into the university network. Using an e-mail package such as Microsoft Outlook (see Figure 70), I would compose a letter and then send it to **president@whitehouse.gov**. The letter would be placed on CCUnet, a network that connects computers on CCU's four campus locations. CCUnet is connected to a nationwide network called PSInet. PSInet would then hand off the letter to a National Science Foundation supercomputer center. From there, the letter would shoot across the NSFnet backbone to a supercomputer center on the east coast, zip through a maze of connections, and finally land in a computer in the White House. The next time the president logged into a White House computer, he would see a note (called a message header) on his display screen indicating that he had new e-mail. The header would list the name of the sender, the subject

of the letter, and the time and date the letter was sent. By double clicking on the header, the president could open the e-mail correspondence and read it.

This global communications network consists of copper telephone lines, fiber optic cables, microwaves, and even satellites orbiting the earth, yet the message arrives at the correct location in seconds. Amazing!

New Internet users are quickly being besieged with a load of jargon and obscure terms. Some of the more important terms and concepts are described here.

A mailing list, or *listserve,* is a list of users and their e-mail addresses. If you are a member of a listserve, every time someone sends something to the list, you get a copy of the message automatically.

Transmission control protocol (TCP) is a means for packaging data. The Internet protocol (IP) places transmissions into *packets* of no more than 1,500 bytes (characters). For larger transmissions, TCP takes over by breaking information into pieces. Each piece is assigned a number so the transmission can be reassembled accurately on the receiving end. TCP/IP are the two main protocols, or rules, that govern how transmissions are handled on the Internet.

Telnet is software that connects a local computer to a remote host computer. The local computer then acts as a terminal connected to the host. To use Telnet, you would type a command in this form at the local computer: **telnet host.subdomain.domain**. For example, the command **telnet ruth.ccu.edu** would connect you with Ruth, the online library card catalog of Colorado Christian University. This would allow you to sit at your local computer and access information on library holdings just as though you were physically located in the CCU library located in Lakewood, Colorado.

File transfer protocol (FTP) enables you to take information you have found on remote computers and download it (copy it) to your local computer. To use FTP, you type a command in this form at the local computer: **ftp host.subdomain.domain**. For example, the command **ftp job.ccu.edu** would connect you with the technical support computer (called Job) at Colorado Christian University where you could download (FTP) many technical files for your use. Both Telnet and FTP require that you have an account on the remote host computer, and the remote host computer must authenticate you through its own security system before allowing you to remotely log on.

Usenet is a separate computer network to which most Internet users have access. Similar to a giant bulletin board, Usenet is used for exchanging articles of common interest. Almost any topic can be found in the over 25,000 topical discussion groups (called newsgroups) which contain messages from people all over the world. You can view replies to these messages to follow the flow of the discussion.

Unlike Usenet, *Internet Relay Chat (IRC)* enables you to join *real-time* discussion groups with other Internet users. This interchange is text-based, meaning that when you type a message, everyone in the group sees it immediately. People reply to your message and soon you are pulled into the conversation exchanging real-time typed messages. If you wish to talk to someone privately you can "whisper" so that only that person can see your message. To initiate a "whispered" message, simply select the name of the person you want to whisper to and type your message. When you click on the whisper button only the intended recipient will be able to view your message.

With *Internet telephony*, you can use the Internet much like a telephone. In fact, your calls are free—even for long distance. To "call" someone, you must identify that the computer of the person you are calling is currently turned on and that his or her Internet telephony software is activated. The "phone" then rings on the other person's end and he or she may choose to answer the call or leave it unanswered. Since this person can see who is calling via Internet caller ID, the decision to answer will be based largely on whether or not the person wishes to talk to you. To answer, the person called can merely click on a button and begin speaking into the microphone. You do the same and carry on a voice conversation. If both computers are equipped with video cameras, you can carry on a conversation while looking at one another's image on your display screen.

The *World Wide Web (WWW)* is a service and set of tools that links huge portions of the Internet. To use the web, you need a program called a browser; *browsers* display web pages. On most web pages, you will see colored and underlined text, called *hyperlinks*, that you can click on to navigate to a different location in the same page or to a completely different page altogether. That other page might be on the same server computer or a completely different server somewhere else around the world.

A *web page* is a single document on the web. Some web pages are very long and some are very short. You can scroll though longer web pages to see all of the information. Most web pages fill up about two screens of text and graphics images.

A *web site* is merely a collection of web pages. Web sites have unique Internet addresses. Most web sites contain dozens or hundreds of web pages. These web pages are linked together though hyperlinks.

The term *home page* essentially means the top-level page of any web site. Most well-designed home pages are brief and offer different hypertext links (linked jump points) to various information resources within that web site.

A *web server* is a program that serves requests from browsers for a particular web page. The server opens up the web page for the requester and then waits for more requests. If the server can't find the requested page, it will send the requestor an error message (which usually reads "HTTP/1.0 404 Object Not Found).

With *browser software*, the Web transforms the normally text-based Internet into a global information system of multimedia richness. The two most popular browsers are Netscape's Navigator and Microsoft's Internet Explorer. Figure 74 shows examples of both of the most popular Internet browsers. (These browser packages can be downloaded for free from either corporate web site.) With the aid of a web browser, you can easily "surf" the World Wide Web to gather information from servers located all over the world. These web servers collectively house an estimated 75 million information resources including text, pictures, sounds, and videos. The major advantage of the World Wide Web is its strengths in dealing with graphical information. For example, you can connect with a computer in France to see paintings from the Louvre Museum, or you can see fossils at UC Berkeley's Paleontology Museum. You can even navigate to the NASA Space Center to check out what's new with the space shuttle or the Hubble Space Telescope (see Figure 75).

The Internet is growing faster than any telecommunications system ever built, including the telephone system. As of October 1993, there were 15 million users. According to recent estimates, the Internet currently has about 75 million users in 132 countries worldwide. Although it is only a subset of the Internet, the World Wide Web is the fastest growing portion of this worldwide telecommunications network. Figure 76 shows a graphical representation of the explosive growth of the Internet and the World Wide Web.

Figure 74 (at left) Internet browser homepages of the two most popular browsers: (a) Microsoft Internet Explorer and (b) Netscape Communicator.

Figure 75 NASA's Hubble space telescope home page.

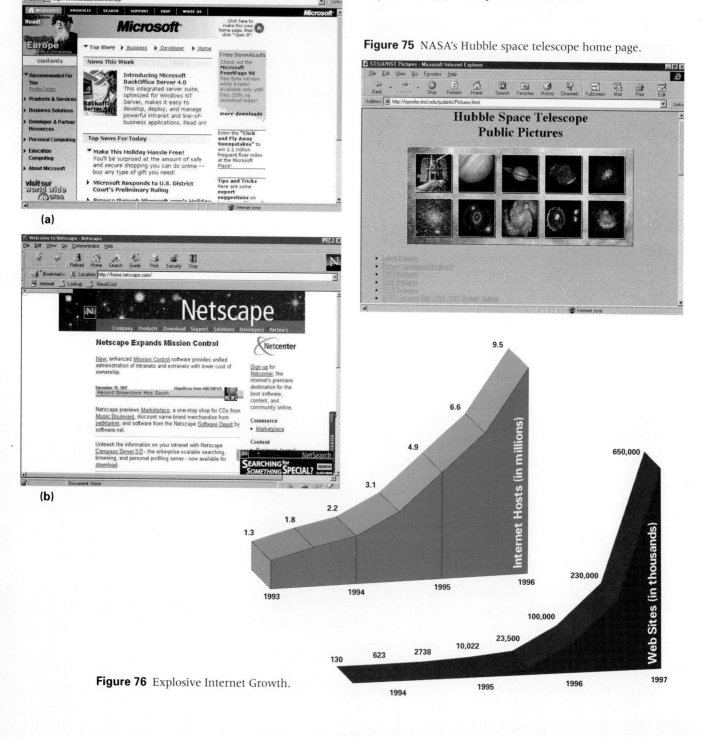

Figure 76 Explosive Internet Growth.

What's in Store for Tomorrow?

The entire computer industry is just over 50 years old. In this brief period of time a great deal of progress has been made. The first computer (the *ENIAC*) took two years to build (see Figure 77). It could make 5,000 calculations per second. ENIAC weighed 30 tons, and was 100 feet long, 10 feet high, and 3 feet deep. ENIAC could store two kilobytes of internal memory and used so much electrical power that it caused the lights to dim in half of Philadelphia when it was powered up. Today, small notebook computers have far more power and capability than ENIAC.

The general trend of easier-to-use, smaller, faster, and cheaper computers will continue into the foreseeable future. Computer chip capacities have been growing at exponential rates over the past couple of decades while integrated circuits are becomming smaller. Figure 78 shows how tiny microprocessors are becoming. Figure 79 shows how fast secondary storage capacity is growing.

In the short term, software will become larger, more powerful, and far easier to use. Hardware will employ *plug-and-play* technology, in which computer equipment can be easily added. The data communications infrastructure will expand (see Figure 80).

The interface with new software applications (and operating systems) will become more intuitive. Online context-sensitive help will assist you in both learning the software and in solving problems. The *interface* will move more toward full integration with speech, so that the computer will actually follow human voice commands.

With new plug-and-play technology, you will simply insert hardware and software components into your computer system. The component will identify itself to the rest of the computer and will tell the computer which resources it requires. The system software will automatically set up a suitable configuration for the new component to ensure that it works

Figure 77 The ENIAC, 1946.

Figure 78 An Intel Pentium processor chip shown on a flower to put its small size in perspective.

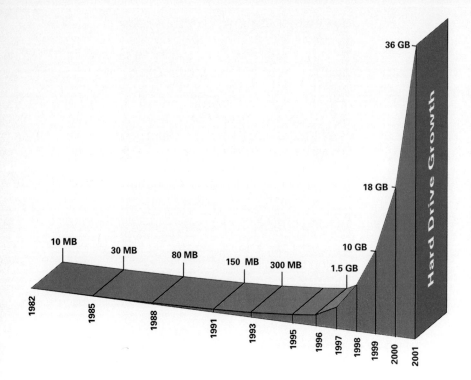
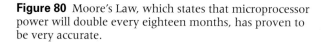
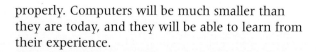

Figure 79 Hard disk drive capacity has increased dramatically to meet the demand of growing operating systems and applications software. This trend will continue.

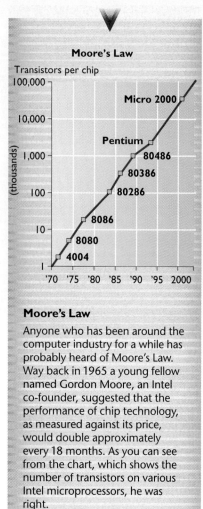

Moore's Law

Anyone who has been around the computer industry for a while has probably heard of Moore's Law. Way back in 1965 a young fellow named Gordon Moore, an Intel co-founder, suggested that the performance of chip technology, as measured against its price, would double approximately every 18 months. As you can see from the chart, which shows the number of transistors on various Intel microprocessors, he was right.

Figure 80 Moore's Law, which states that microprocessor power will double every eighteen months, has proven to be very accurate.

properly. Computers will be much smaller than they are today, and they will be able to learn from their experience.

Currently the U.S. government and private industry are investing billions of dollars to replace traditional copper communications lines with fiber optic cables that can simultaneously carry telephone calls, television signals, and two-way computer transmissions. In addition, wireless networking technologies that carry all kinds of information are rapidly emerging.

Perhaps the biggest impending trend of change in technology has to do with the *convergence* of media. We call this trend *digital convergence.* When you think about it, all media is becoming digitized. The reason you can buy a *New York Times* newspaper in the city of Denver is not because a high-flying paperboy delivered it. The reason is because it was created in a digital form. All of the words and all of

the pictures in that newspaper are made up of bits. Information in the form of bits can be easily sent from computer to computer. Like the print media industry, digitization is occurring in the entertainment industry as well. Music is now published on CDs and movies are now being distributed on DVDs. Television and radio are now being broadcast in digital form. Telephones are becoming digital.

Because all of these technologies are converging around digital media, this means that these technologies can be "viewed" and processed by computers. This continuing trend toward convergence is causing the lines between computers, communications, entertainment, and publishing to become blurred. All areas of life—education, business, communication, entertainment—as we know them today will be radically affected. Even the role of the familiar public library will change. Because of the relentless evolutions (and perhaps revolutions) in computer technologies and digital convergence of information, new technological solutions (and problems) will become realities. Figure 81 illustrates this digital convergence. You'll be able to access that information from just about anywhere at any time as is demonstrated in Figure 82. In short, computers and computer-based technology will become ubiquitous.

Predicting the future is never easy. Nobody guessed that a meager bit of sand in the form of a silicon chip would transform the world. Silicon chips form the core of computers and are so pervasive that you hardly notice that they are there. From automated teller machines to electronic cash registers, computers are not only making mundane tasks easier, but are giving us new opportunities that would be impossible without them. Medicine, architecture, cinema, and business are just a few of the fields in which computers have become an integral part of everyday life. Many argue that no field of endeavor has been left unchanged by the computer revolution. Like it or not, how far you go in your chosen career may very well depend upon how well you use a computer.

Figure 81 All media is converging around digital transmission and distribution.

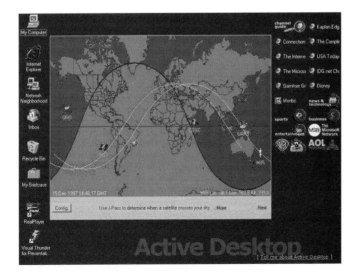

Figure 82 The channels in the upper right corner are active links to the Internet that, when clicked, immediately connect you to the new information gathered. The map is actually an active link to the Internet that tracks the locations of several key satellites that are currently orbiting the earth.

Computers and Society

Over the course of history many breakthroughs in technology have led to major societal changes. Whether we talk about the technology of domesticating animals, which brought on the agricultural age, or the technology of the power-loom for producing cloth and textiles, which brought on the industrial age, society has been inalterably changed by technological innovation. Today's technologies no less affect society than those of yesterday. In fact, it can be argued that information technology is having a profound impact on all areas of society and that impact is "snowballing." Like all technological impacts these changes can be viewed as both positive and negative. Although using modern information technologies presents tremendous opportunities, there is also significant potential for problems.

 FYI "Concerns for man and his fate must always form the chief interest of all technological endeavors. Never forget this in the midst of your diagrams and equations."
—Albert Einstein

Information technology can have a very liberating impact on society. An example is the working professional who can "attend" classes in a virtual sense without leaving home. In this manner, one can pursue a dream of higher education yet meet the many daily demands of career and family at the same time. Yet this same technology can have an alienating effect, becuase the virtual student has less face-to-face contact with fellow students and their professors.

A key strategy in "steering" the impact of technology on our lives lies in accepting the fact that these technologies are real, and they are here to stay. Once we accept this, we can also embrace the notion that as members of an increasingly technological society, we must understand the power of technology and its inherent limitations in order to use it wisely. We need to remember that any technology that can be used can also be abused.

Change Is Not What It Used To Be

Civilization as we know it is in the midst of a global transformation from an industrial economy to an information economy. This massive shift is influencing the way we live, work, learn, and play. It will likely challenge many of our current beliefs, traditions, and foundational assumptions.

Our ancestors spent an enormous amount of time and energy creating clothing, shelter, and food. Advancing technologies have cut the time and effort we spend on these efforts and have paid rich dividends, such as improved health care, better nutrition, and cleaner sanitation. Thanks to science and technology, we are now the healthiest and longest-living people in human history. But technology's positive benefits have many negative side effects, such as the threat of global warfare, a damaged ecosystem, and tremendous occupational and economic shifts.

The computer industry recently turned 50 years old. In that brief period of time, technology has radically advanced and has, indeed, turned the world inside out. In fact, if we were still required to use vacuum tube technology (as with the ENIAC), the processing power of a common Pentium microprocessor would need a computer the size of the United States Pentagon.

We are now approaching what will probably be the greatest acceleration in the rate of technological development the world has ever known. In speculating about the next 50 years of computing, National Medal of Technology winner Gordon Bell said, "If hardware (such as semiconductors, magnetic memories, and fiber optics) continues to evolve at the annual factor of 1.60 rate we know as Moore's Law, then computers that are 10 billion times more powerful will exist!"

As these new technologies come into being they will have a profound effect on society and humankind. Although the rate of technological change is relatively easy to predict, the specific technological leaps are yet to be imagined. These tremendous technological advances will spread throughout society like ripples on a pond and the new "networked world" will ensure that those ripples continue to spread at an ever faster rate. In his book, *Growing Up Digital*, Don Tapscott stated, "The Net is beginning to affect all of us—the way we create wealth, the enterprise, the nature of commerce and marketing, the delivery system for entertainment and the role and dynamics of learning in the economy, the nature of government and governance, our culture, and arguably the role of the nation-state in the body politic."

Our newly "wired planet" is forming a new way to communicate and live. It looks promising, but perhaps we should think about some of the unanticipated side effects of these new technologies. The technology of television has produced a number of unintended side effects (perhaps even an increase in violence and promiscuity). There is reason for concern about the unforeseen results of our new global communications network. Disney Fellow Alan Kay made the point, "Much care has to be taken … in order for this change to be positive. We don't have natural defenses against fat, sugar, salt, alcohol, alkaloids—or media. Television should be the last mass communications medium to be naively designed and put into the world without a surgeon general's warning!"

Nothing better characterizes our day and age than the rapid pace of accelerated change. Such change often confronts us with ethical challenges. For example, modern medical technologies have begun to force us to grapple with the ethical dilemmas of patient rights and even the right to die. Modern technology provides enormous power—for good or evil. Technology itself is morally neutral. How we use the technology is the heart of the issue. A hammer is neither good nor bad. It can be used to build a house or it can be used as a gruesome weapon. As with any powerful tool, the power of advanced technology must be balanced with responsible use.

The ever-increasing pace of technological change demands that we gain deeper insight into the ethical implications of creating and using new technologies. We must individually and collectively wrestle with the myriad ethical issues we face, including privacy versus freedom of information, data regulation, computer liability, intellectual property rights, and technology access for all.

FYI "We should all be concerned about the future because we will have to spend the rest of our lives there."

—Charles Kettering

Summary and Exercises

Summary

- The tangible equipment within a computer system is called hardware.
- A typical personal computer system includes a monitor, mouse, keyboard, printer, modem, and software.
- The sequenced, step-by-step instructions that instruct a computer are called software.
- A computer is an electronic device capable of storing, retrieving, and processing data.
- The processor or central processing unit (CPU) processes raw data into useful information.
- The four main components of the computer system are input, processing, output, and secondary storage. These four main components are illustrated in the IPOS cycle.
- Secondary storage is auxiliary storage that is used to more permanently store data to be processed by the CPU.
- Computers can be categorized by size: supercomputers, mainframes, minicomputers, and microcomputers.
- The three main categories of software are operating systems, applications software, and programming languages.
- The group of programs that supervise and coordinate the operations of a computer system is known as an operating system.
- Easy-to-use graphical user interfaces (GUI), such as Windows 95 and the Macintosh OS, replaced command line interface for PCs.
- Application software refers to software that helps people solve particular problems such as creating a term paper, developing a budget, or charting profits.
- Communications software allows the end user to connect two or more computers together (usually via the telephone lines) in order to share data and information.
- Each 1 or 0 in the computer is called a bit (binary digit).
- A group of eight bits, which represents one character, is called a byte.
- Random access memory (RAM) is where data and instructions are held temporarily for processing.
- Computer speeds are usually represented in megahertz (MHz), which represent millions of machine cycles per second.
- The keyboard is the most common input device used for computers.

- The mouse is an input device that, when rolled on the surface of a desk, translates its movements into corresponding movements of a pointer on the screen.
- The monitor is the primary output device for computers. Output to a computer screen is known as soft copy (unlike hard copy, which is produced on paper).
- Printers produce output on paper or other physical media.
- Secondary storage is storage that is separate from the primary memory of the computer.
- Diskettes and hard disk drives are magnetic media that represent data in the form of magnetized spots on a disk, with the presence of a magnetized spot representing a 1 and a nonmagnetized spot representing a 0.
- Optical disk technology uses a laser beam to enter (and read) data in the form of microscopic spots.
- Multimedia software usually represents information with text, graphics, photos, narration, music, animation, and full-motion video.
- Modems are telecommunications devices that translate digital information (from computers) to analog information (carried by the telephone system) and vice versa.
- A protocol is a set of rules for exchanging data between computers.
- The protocol that makes the Internet possible is called transmission control protocol/Internet protocol (TCP/IP).
- Networks are interconnected collections of computers that share hardware, software, and data.
- Networks can be classified as local area networks (LANs) and wide area networks (WANs).
- A local area network (LAN) is usually made up of computers that share information within a building or small campus.
- A wide area network (WAN) is a network of geographically separated computers.
- The Internet (the world's biggest WAN) is a worldwide collection of both large and small networks that connects universities, government agencies, military sites, public organizations, and private companies.
- The World Wide Web (WWW) is a subset of the Internet that utilizes linked text and pictures to navigate from Internet site to Internet site. These links are called hypertext links.
- In the future, computers will become smaller and yet more powerful.
- Any technology that can be used can also be abused.

Study Questions _____

Multiple Choice

1. Which of the following is not an example of a hardware category?
   a. input
   b. processing
   c. format
   d. output

2. The microprocessor is an example of
   a. a program.
   b. an input device.
   c. hardware.
   d. software.

3. The step-by-step instructions that govern the computer are called
   a. hardware.
   b. software.
   c. input.
   d. output.

4. Printers and display screens are forms of
   a. input devices.
   b. output devices.
   c. storage devices.
   d. processing devices.

5. Software used to access the World Wide Web is called
   a. a browser.
   b. a server.
   c. e-mail.
   d. Usenet news.

6. The software that serves the computer's needs is called
   a. applications.
   b. the operating system.
   c. shareware.
   d. groupware.

7. Software that serves specific work-related needs for people is called
   a. applications.
   b. the operating system.
   c. shareware.
   d. groupware.

8. Software that enables end users to produce professional newsletters and reports is called
   a. database management.
   b. spreadsheets.
   c. graphics.
   d. desktop publishing.

9. Which of the following is not an example of application software?
   a. Novell NetWare
   b. Microsoft Word
   c. Aldus Freehand
   d. Microsoft Paintbrush

10. Software that enables end users to manipulate numbers in a row and column format is called
    a. database management.
    b. spreadsheets.
    c. graphics.
    d. desktop publishing.

11. AutoCAD is a
    a. special computer system for automobiles.
    b. vector graphics drawing program.
    c. database management system similar to dBase IV.
    d. CPU manufacturer.

12. Equal to, not equal to, less than, and greater than are examples of
    a. logical operations.
    b. cerulean operators.
    c. arithmetic operations.
    d. memory registers.

13. Computer operations are synchronized by
    a. the binary system.
    b. the disk drive.
    c. the CPU clock.
    d. the modem.

14. The random access memory (RAM) capacity in personal computers is usually expressed in
    a. kilobytes.
    b. megabytes.
    c. gigabytes.
    d. terabytes.

15. Megahertz are used to measure
    a. disk access time.
    b. keyboard input speed.
    c. CPU clock speed.
    d. mouse speed.

16. A pictorial screen symbol that represents a computer resource is known as
  a. a pointer.
  b. an icon.
  c. a trackball.
  d. a graphic.

17. With Kodak's Photo CD system,
  a. you can stick blank CDs into a special digital camera called Kodak's CD PhotoMate.
  b. you can store about 100 photos.
  c. you can erase old photos from CDs and replace them with new ones.
  d. none of the above

18. The name for the clarity of the screen (or printer) is called
  a. pixelation.
  b. discretion.
  c. resolution.
  d. dot intensity.

19. LCDs are well suited for portable computers because
  a. they are flat.
  b. they consume little power.
  c. they are lightweight.
  d. all of the above

20. On a magnetic storage medium, a magnet spot represents
  a. a zero bit.
  b. a one bit.
  c. a megabit.
  d. a megahertz.

21. A collection of eight bits is called a
  a. file.
  b. byte.
  c. megabyte.
  d. data bit.

22. The protocol used by all computers using the Internet is called
  a. LAN.
  b. WAN.
  c. EDI.
  d. TCP/IP.

23. The Internet is managed by
  a. the Federal Communications Commission (FCC).
  b. the National Science Foundation (NSF).
  c. no one.
  d. the Advanced Research projects Agency (ARPA).

24. Which of the following is an example of a commercial information service?
  a. Ethernet
  b. America Online
  c. AppleTalk
  d. all of the above

25. Computer signals that are to be transmitted over telephone lines must first be converted to
  a. modem lines.
  b. microwaves.
  c. digital signals.
  d. analog signals.

Short Answer

1. What are the major elements in the IPOS cycle?

2. A computer has 8 MB of RAM. What does this mean?

3. Is Windows 98 a complete operating system? Explain why or why not.

4. A computer user has the Internet address **garyewen@ccu.edu**. Explain each part of this address.

5. Explain how dot pitch affects screen resolution.

6. List four applications software packages and briefly describe how each is used.

7. Describe how computers are classified by size. What are the different sizes? What kind are you most likely to use?

8. What is a software suite and what is the advantage of buying one?

9. Why is a Pentium-based CPU better than the CPU found in the original IBM PC?

10. You are going to scan your resume to edit it within Microsoft Word. What hardware and software will you need to successfully scan the text in a form suitable for a word processor?

True/False

1. The Internet is a subset of the World Wide Web.

2. The entity that supplies access to the Internet is called an internet service provider (ISP).

3. Secondary storage is another name for RAM.

4. A LAN usually connects cities in different states.

5. A computer operating system is an example of applications software.

6. Secondary storage holds data in a volatile fashion.

7. An internal clock produces pulses at a fixed rate in order to synchronize computer operations.

8. A byte is commonly made up of eight bits.

9. A bit is commonly made up of eight bytes.

10. Random access memory is volatile.

11. The greater the number of dots, the better the resolution.

12. CD-R technology permits writing data onto CD-ROMs.

13. Multimedia software can include full motion video sequences.

14. Local area networks are designed to connect computers in the same geographical location.

15. In order to navigate to a new site, a user of the World Wide Web must type in the site's URL.

Fill-In

1. The four general hardware classifications within a computer system are
   a. _____
   b. _____
   c. _____
   d. _____

2. CPU stands for _____.

3. Another name for a personal computer is _____.

4. The CPU processes data into _____ .

5. MHz is an abbreviation for _____ .

6. RAM stands for _____ .

7. The pictorial screen symbol that represents computer resources is called _____ .

8. What computer hardware device converts digital signals to analog and back again? _____

9. A set of established rules for exchanging data between computers is called _____ .

10. The first page of a web site is called _____ .

You Decide

1. You are going back in time with a portable computer to meet Leonardo da Vinci. What software would you recommend for him to paint the Mona Lisa? Why? What software would you recommend to him to draw an airplane? Why?

2. A small college has hired you to install PCs for all employees. Should you network the computers? Perhaps some need to be networked and some don't. What are the advantages and costs involved? Are there disadvantages?

3. You have been hired by a shoe manufacturer to create a brochure describing their products. You don't have a computer, but the manufacturer will buy you one. What kind of computer will you buy? What kind of CPU will it have? How much RAM and hard disk space will you need? Will you get a mouse and a modem? Will you need a laser printer or perhaps a color ink jet printer? What software should you buy? Explain your answers.

4. Because you are quickly becoming a PC guru, you have been asked by the President of the United States to provide your vision of the future of computing. What do you think will be the short-term (in the next 5 to 10 years) developments in hardware and software? What about long-term developments (over the next 50 years)?

For Discussion

1. Why is giving instructions to a computer more difficult than giving instructions to a human being?

2. In light of emerging technologies, is the continued practice of learning keyboarding skills worthwhile? Why?

3. Discuss the advantages and disadvantages of telecommuting.

4. How might digital convergence impact society? Explain.

5. How might information technology be abused in the future? What can be done to prevent such abuse?

Glossary

access time Measurement of the time it takes to find the track and then the sector that contains desired data on a disk. Measured in milliseconds.

ALU *See* arithmetic and logic unit.

America Online (AOL) A major online information service that offers a wide variety of services and Internet access.

analog signal The electrical signal used to represent data over phone lines. Often associated with sounds.

application software Software that helps solve a particular problem. Performs specific tasks, such as creating a term paper, developing a budget, or charting profits.

arithmetic and logic unit (ALU) Part of the central processing unit that handles math and logic functions.

ASCII (American Standard Code for Information Interchange) A binary coding scheme that uses eight-bit segments of 1s and 0s to represent data characters.

assembly language A programming language one step above machine language. Difficult to use.

backbone The major communication lines that tie networks together.

bandwidth The carrying capacity of a communications medium.

BASIC (Beginners' All-purpose Symbolic Instruction Code) A popular programming language used mainly for teaching purposes.

baud rate The speed at which data is transmitted by a modem over telephone lines. *See* bits per second.

bit Short for binary digit, the smallest unit of information in a computer. Represented by either a 1 or a 0.

bitmapped graphics Graphics created by painting software. With bitmapped graphics, a pointing device—a mouse, a trackball, or a pen on a pressure-sensitive tablet—is used to manipulate individual pixels on a computer screen.

bits per second (bps) The rate at which data transmission speeds are measured through networks and telecommunications systems.

booting Loading the operating system into random access memory (RAM).

bps *See* bits per second.

browser Software used to access and navigate the Internet.

bus network A network that has a single line to which all networked devices are attached.

byte (B) A group of eight bits. Roughly equivalent to one character of data, such as a letter, a number, or a special character.

C A programming language originally developed for writing operating systems. Its high degree of sophistication has made it a popular language for developing new application software at companies such as Lotus, Microsoft, and Borland.

C++ An object-oriented programming language based on the C programming language.

CAD *See* computer-aided design.

carrier sense multiple access with collision detect (CSMA/CD) A transmission strategy in an Ethernet network where each computer is "listening" to the cable, waiting for a break in the network traffic before sending out data. If two computers try to send data at the same time, a collision occurs. Then each computer waits a preset amount of time before attempting to retransmit data.

cathode ray tube (CRT) A TV-style screen used in most desk-top computers. Works by shooting an electron beam out of the back of a picture tube. When the beam strikes the front of the tube, tiny dots of phosphor called pixels are lit up. Characters and graphical images are created by patterns of pixels.

CD-R A technology that allows writing (recording) data to optical disks.

CD-ROM *See* compact disk-read-only memory.

cell The intersection of a row and column in a spreadsheet. Data is entered into individual cells.

central processing unit (CPU) The chip in a computer that interprets and executes program instructions.

character A letter, number, or special character that can be entered from the keyboard.

charting software Application software that enables a user to visually display data (often spreadsheet data) to help in decision making. Part of spreadsheet software packages such as Lotus 1-2-3 and Microsoft Excel.

chip A small, rectangular piece of silicon—an element extracted from sand—that contains thousands of circuits.

click To press and quickly release the mouse button. Used to choose commands or select text.

client Another term for a workstation in a network, which is typically a microcomputer. A program on a local computer that allows that node to communicate with the central server.

clock speed The speed at which the computer's internal clock synchronizes computer operations, measured in megahertz (MHz).

coaxial cable A cable similar to the cable that connects a TV to cable TV systems. Used to connect computers in a network.

COBOL (COmmon Business-Oriented Language) A relatively old programming language still used for many business applications.

command-line interface   A user interface that requires the user to remember and type each command precisely.

compact disk-read-only memory (CD-ROM)   A 12-centimeter disk that can store up to 680 megabytes of text, animation, video clips, graphics, and sound. A laser reads the data, which is permanently stored as microscopic cavities on the disk's surface.

computer   An electronic device capable of storing, retrieving, and processing data.

computer-aided design (CAD)   Drawing software used by architects and engineers for their designs.

computer literacy   The awareness, knowledge of, and ability to interact with computers.

computer programmer   A person who designs, writes, and tests computer programs.

computer system   A group of computer-related parts brought together to form a unified whole for the purpose of processing data.

copyrighted software   Software designed, programmed, and packaged as an intellectual property. Good software is expensive to create and must not be copied without permission from the manufacturer.

CPU   *See* central processing unit.

CRT   *See* cathode ray tube.

CSMA/CD   *See* carrier sense multiple access with collision detect.

data   Raw facts, figures, or characters that are processed by application software.

data bus   The cables that carry data from the CPU to RAM and to the other components of the computer.

data communications   The process of sending and receiving data over telecommunications facilities.

data transfer rate   The speed, measured in kilobytes per second, at which data is read from a disk. A very important characteristic of a CD-ROM drive.

database   A highly structured collection of data, such as a warehouse inventory list or a mailing list.

database management system (DBMS)   Application software that enables a user to manipulate a database. Often used to sort delete, update, and summarize data.

DBMS   *See* database management system.

demodulate   The translation by modems of analog signals into digital signals for the purpose of reconstructing the original digital message after analog transmission.

desktop   In a graphical operating environment, the screen background that serves as a graphics-based work area.

desktop publishing software   Application software used for creating professional-looking newsletters, brochures, and reports.

digital signal   The electrical signal of distinct on (1) and off (0) impulses used to represent data in computers.

digital versatile disk (DVD)   A form of optical disk storage capable of storing more data than a typical CD-ROM.

digitizing tablet   A graphics input device in the form of a flat membrane with a special stylus used to draw or trace images.

disk   *See* floppy disk; hard disk.

disk drive   A device into which a floppy disk fits or in which a hard disk is housed. Contains the read/write head and other mechanisms for reading and writing data.

diskette   A single disk made of mylar on which data is recorded as magnetic spots.

disk operating system (DOS)   Prior to the release of Windows 95, the most popular operating system for IBM PCs and compatibles.

domain   The name of an Internet service provider as it appears in the Internet address (URL).

DOS *See* disk operating system.

DOS prompt   A marker on the screen (usually something like **C:\>**) that indicates DOS is ready to accept a typed command.

DOS shell   A menu-driven interface for DOS. Makes DOS commands much easier to run but still needs DOS to run.

dot matrix printer   An impact printer whose print mechanism contains 9 to 24 tiny hammers or pins that strike the printer ribbon, which then hits the paper to produce characters and graphics. Better resolution is obtained by having more pins or by performing multiple passes across the paper. The printers are relatively inexpensive, but often loud and slow.

dot pitch   The distance in millimeters (mm) between adjacent pixels on a screen. Measurements such as .28mm or .39mm are typical; the smaller the distance, the better the screen resolution.

dots per inch (dpi)   An expression used to measure the resolution of printed output. The more dots an image contains, the sharper it appears to the eye.

download   The act of receiving copies of files on a local computer from a host computer.

DVD   *See* digital versatile disk.

dpi   *See* dots per inch.

drawing software   Application software that creates vector graphics. All drawn objects are stored as mathematical formulas that describe their shape, size, and color.

electronic data interchange (EDI)   A set of standards by which companies can electronically exchange business-related information.

electronic fund transfer (EFT) Paying for goods and services by transferring funds electronically.

electronic mail (e-mail) Mail sent digitally from computer to computer over telecommunications lines or direct network connections.

electronic spreadsheet A computerized worksheet used to organize data into row and column format.

e-mail *See* electronic mail.

end user The person who ultimately uses the computer or software.

ENIAC (Electronic Numerical Integrator And Computer) The first general-purpose electronic computer, built by John Mauchly and J. Presper Eckert, Jr. First used in 1946.

Ethernet A popular communications standard for transporting data throughout a computer network.

fiber optic cable A thin glass fiber that carries digital signals as pulses of light.

fiber optics Technology that uses glass fibers that transmit light impulses to represent data.

file A program or set of data with a unique name.

file compression A method of reducing the size of a file by using fewer bits to represent the data. To recreate the original data, the file must be decompressed.

file server The central server in a network that provides multi-user access to programs and data.

file transfer protocol (FTP) Internet-based software that enables a user to take information found on remote computers and copy it to a local computer.

flatbed scanner A desktop scanning device that can scan a sheet of paper (or bound document) to input either text or graphics into the computer.

floppy disk A flat round disk of mylar that is used to store data in the form of magnetic spots.

format The act of placing tracks, sectors, and other organizational components onto the surface of a disk so that it can be used to store data. *See* initialize.

FORTRAN (FORmula TRANslator) A programming language used primarily for engineering and scientific applications.

FTP *See* file transfer protocol.

GB *See* gigabyte.

giga (G) A prefix that represents approximately one billion. Used primarily for measuring computer memory and secondary storage capacity.

gigabyte (GB) One billion bytes.

Gopher An program developed at the University of Minnesota that enables users to browse Internet resources represented by a series of menus.

graphical user interface (GUI) An easy-to-use communications system between a user and a computer. Usually includes windows, icons, pull-down menus, and a pointer controlled by a pointing device such as a mouse.

groupware Software that helps groups of people collaborate to develop or track a project, usually including electronic mail, networking, and database applications.

GUI *See* graphical user interface.

handheld scanner A small scanning device that can be passed over a sheet of paper (or bound document) to input either text or graphics into the computer.

hard copy Tangible, long-term output such as that produced by printers.

hard disk A secondary storage medium usually made of rigid aluminum or glass that stores large quantities of data by virtue of magnetic spots.

hardware The tangible equipment (display screen, keyboard, printer, and other related parts) that makes up the computer system.

head crash The violate collision of a read/write head and a hard disk surface, usually caused by a sudden vibration. Often results in inability to recover some or all of the data stored on the disk.

high-level language An English-like programming language that is easier to use than older symbolic languages (such as machine language).

home page The first (or initial) page of a web site.

host computer The central computer in a network to which other computers attach in order to share resources.

hub A device that physically connects two or more cables in a network.

hyperlink The text or graphic image (on the World Wide Web) that can be clicked to initiate a link to a different information resource.

hypertext The text (on the World Wide Web) that can be clicked to initiate a link to a different information resource. Hypertext is usually identified by a different color and may be underlined.

icon A small pictorial representation of a computer resource as presented in a windows-based (GUI) interface.

impact printer A printer whose print mechanism actually impresses the printer ribbon against the surface of the paper.

information Processed data that has meaning and can be used for some purpose.

initialize A term used, usually on a Macintosh, for preparing a disk for storing data. *See* format.

ink-jet printer A nonimpact printer that sprays droplets of ink from multiple nozzles onto paper to create characters or graphics.

input The act of entering raw data into a computer system for processing.

input device Any hardware device used to enter raw data into a computer system for processing.

integrated software An applications program that usually includes word processing, spreadsheets, database manager, and graphics programs all wrapped up into one program package. Microsoft Works and ClarisWorks are good examples.

Internet A worldwide network of networks, large and small, that connects universities, government agencies, military sites, public organizations, and private companies.

Internet protocol (IP)   A communications standard in which a computer places data into an electronic envelope (called a packet) before sending the data.

IP   *See* Internet protocol.

internet service provider (ISP)   An organization that offers, for a fee, a connection to the Internet.

ISP   *See* Internet service provider.

keyboard   The most common input device for entering data into a computer. Similar to a typewriter keyboard but usually includes other additional keys for performing specific computer-related tasks.

kilobyte (KB)   One thousand bytes.

kilo (K)   A prefix that represents approximately one thousand. Used primarily for measuring computer memory and secondary storage capacity.

LAN   *See* local area network.

land   A microscopic flat spot on the surface of a CD-ROM. Used in conjunction with pits to represent 0s and 1s.

laptop computer   A small portable computer, usually somewhat larger than a notebook computer.

laser printer   A type of nonimpact printer that uses a light beam, a technology similar to that used in copier machines, to create printed images quickly and quietly.

LCD   *See* liquid crystal display.

liquid crystal display (LCD)   A flat, lightweight video display that consumes little power and is well-suited for portable computers.

local area network (LAN)   A network of computers that connects a group of computers (usually confined to a common building).

machine language   A very low-level programming language, which consists of 1s and 0s, that works directly with the computer (on the computer's level).

MacOS   The Apple Macintosh operating system. *See* operating system.

magnetic disk   A type of secondary storage that is used in either a floppy disk or hard disk. Used to store programs and data.

magnetic tape   A type of secondary storage made of a ribbon of mylar that is wound on reels contained in plastic cassettes as small (or smaller) than those used for taping speech and music. Very well suited for making backup copies of information, because large quantities of data can be stored at a very low cost.

main memory   *See* random access memory.

mainframe computer   A powerful, multi-user computer used by banks, airlines, and other large organizations.

MB (megabyte)   One million bytes.

mega   A prefix that represents approximately one million. Used primarily for measuring computer memory and secondary storage capacity.

megahertz (MHz)   Millions of electrical pulses per second to measure the speed of computer components.

memory   The electrical circuitry that temporarily holds data and instructions to be processed by the CPU.

menu   A list of commands from which a user can choose.

menu-driven interface   A user interface in which a user choose a command from a list of commands called a menu.

MHz   *See* megahertz.

microcomputer   A computer used by one person at a time. Ranges in size from a handheld portable to a tower unit that stands on the floor. *See also* personal computer.

microprocessor   The CPU of a microcomputer. Interprets and executes program instructions

microsecond   One millionth of a second.

MIDI   *See* musical instrument digital interface.

millisecond   One thousandth of a second.

minicomputer   A multi-user, scaled-down version of a mainframe. Used by colleges, universities, retail businesses, and government agencies to deliver timesharing capabilities at lower costs than mainframes.

MIPS   Millions of instructions per second. A measure of how fast a computer can calculate.

modem (MOdulator/DEModulator)   Found at the end of a two-computer telecommunications system. Translates, or modulates, the digital signal found in computers into an analog signal, which is carried over phone lines. Also translates, or demodulates, the analog signal from phone lines back into digital pulses.

modulate   The translation by a modem of a digital signal into an analog signal.

monitor   *See* screen.

monochrome graphics   The simplest type of bitmapped graphics. Only lets the user turn pixels on and off.

mouse   An input device with a ball on its underside that detects movement. As the mouse is moved on a flat surface, a pointer on the screen moves in a corresponding direction.

multimedia   A system that involves the interactive use of animation, photos, video, and sound on a computer.

multitasking   An operating system that runs two or more programs simultaneously, with each program running in its own window.

musical instrument digital interface (MIDI)   A musical system that enables electronic instruments, such as electronic keyboards or guitars, to communicate with computers.

Mylar   A flexible material that serves as the medium for floppy disks.

nanosecond   One billionth of a second.

network   A group of two or more computer systems linked together.

network interface card (NIC)   A circuit board that plugs into a computer and serves as a communications interface between the computer and a network.

network operating system (NOS)   An operating system controls and supervises the activities of the network.

NIC   *See* network interface card.

nonimpact printer   A printer that produces output with tiny drops of ink. It is more expensive than impact printers, in general, and produces very high-quality output.

NOS   *See* network operating system.

notebook computer   A portable computer about the size of a notebook.

OCR   *See* optical character recognition.

online   A direct connection from a node to a central server in a data communications environment.

online service   A commercial provider of consumer-oriented information and Internet access (America Online, Microsoft Network, CompuServe) for which a monthly access fee is paid.

operating environment   A work area created on top of the operating system by programs such as Windows. Includes a graphical user interface, multitasking, and the copying and pasting of data.

operating system   A group of programs that supervises and controls the operations of the computer.

optical character recognition (OCR)   Software that "reads" or deciphers individual characters or digits in scanned text.

optical disk   Storage technology based on a laser beam to store large amounts of data.

optical scanner   A light-sensitive input device that enables a computer to *"see"* digitally. Light is reflected off drawings, pictures, or text and then captured using light-sensitive electronics. The captured image appears on the screen.

output   The display of processed data (information) for human consumption.

output device   A device such as a visual display or printer for making processed data (information) available for use.

painting software   An application that produces bitmapped graphics in which a pointing device—a mouse, a trackball, or a pen on a pressure-sensitive tablet—is used to manipulate individual pixels on the screen.

palmtop computer   A portable computer that fits in the palm of your hand.

parallel interface   An all-purpose computer interface that moves data eight bits at a time (limited to distances under 20 feet).

Pascal   A programming language named after the French mathematician Blaise Pascal. Because of its simple approach it is used to teach programming.

PDA   *See* personal digital assistant.

pen-based computer   A computer that accepts input from a stylus applied directly to a flat panel screen. The stylus can be used to enter handwritten text, to draw diagrams, or to point to objects on the screen.

peripheral hardware   All input, output, and secondary storage equipment attached to the computer.

personal computer   A computer used by one person at a time. Ranges in size from a small handheld portable to a tower unit that stands on the floor. *See also* microcomputer.

personal digital assistant (PDA)   An emerging category of pen-based computers that serves as a handheld notebook, an appointment calendar, a drawing pad, and sometimes even a fax machine and cellular phone.

picosecond   One trillionth of a second.

pit   A microscopic cavity in the surface of a CD-ROM. Used to represent bits.

pixel   Short for picture element. Tiny dots of phosphor that are "lit up" on the front of a CRT. Patterns of pixels create characters and graphical images.

plug-and-play   Technology that enables a user to install a card, such as a modem or video card, and then use the card without having to set any jumpers or switches. The card identifies itself to the rest of the computer and tells the computer which resources it requires. The system's software automatically sets up a suitable configuration for the card.

pointer   A screen indicator that represents where the next end-user interaction with the computer will take place.

presentation graphics   Business software for the purpose of creating sophisticated graphs and charts to represent data.

primary memory   *See* random-access memory.

printer   A device used for creating hard-copy output on a piece of paper.

processor   The central processing unit (CPU) of a computer system.

program   A set of step-by-step instructions that controls computer equipment to perform specified tasks. *See also* software.

programming language   Used to write step-by-step instructions, or programs, that control the computer.

quartz crystal   A device that emits electrical pulses that determine how quickly the CPU executes instructions. Similar to a metronome that keeps a pianist in time with his or her music.

RAM   *See* random-access memory.

random-access memory (RAM)   A temporary work area in which application software is used to refine data until it is in its completed form. RAM contents disappear when the computer is turned off.

read-only memory (ROM)   Memory chips that are preprogrammed at the factory to contain data and programs that can be read but not altered in any way. Data and instructions remain in ROM even after power to the computer is disrupted.

read/write head   An electromagnet positioned above or below the surface of a disk for the purpose of magnetizing or demagnetizing spots on the disk.

resolution   The sharpness of a picture image, defined by the total number of pixels and the distance between pixels.

ROM   *See* read-only memory.

scanner   A device that uses a source of light to read text and/or images from hard-copy sources directly into the computer.

screen   A video display unit used to output processed data (information) for human visual study.

scrolling   A feature wherein the user can use the keyboard or pointing device to move a document on the screen for the purpose of viewing any portion.

SCSI (Small Computer Systems Interface)   An all-purpose computer interface noted for its speed of data transfer and its ability to accommodate up to seven devices on one physical port.

secondary storage   Auxiliary storage (often on disk) used to more permanently store data and information to be processed by the CPU.

serial interface   An all-purpose computer interface that moves data one bit at a time.

server   The central computer in a network environment that controls and manages the network and serves files and programs to networked computers.

SIMM (SIMM)   See single in-line memory module.

single in-line memory module (SIMM)   A small circuit board composed of RAM chips.

single-tasking   Type of operating system that runs one application program at a time.

site license   A special software license permitting a customer to make multiple copies of a single piece of software.

soft copy   Visual but intangible computer-produced output displayed temporarily on a visual display screen.

software   Step-by-step sets of instructions that instruct a computer how to operate. Also known as programs.

speech recognition   Type of software application that enables computer systems to recognize spoken words.

software suite   A bundle of comprehensive application programs sold within one package, such as Microsoft Office and Lotus SmartSuite.

sound card   A circuit board that plugs into the main system board of a computer. Gives a computer the ability to generate speech and music through speakers that plug directly into the card. Also accepts a plug-in microphone to record speech or short sound clips.

spreadsheet   A matrix of rows and columns that contains text, numbers, and formulas. Usually used in business applications.

spreadsheet software   Application software that manipulates spreadsheets.

stylus   A pen-shaped input device for a PDA. Has a small, dull point that inputs data into the unit when pressure is applied to the screen.

supercomputer   The most powerful category of computers. Because of their expense, they are used only by large organizations with tremendous data manipulation requirements.

superscalar design   A feature of the Intel Pentium CPU that enables it to process two 32-bit instructions at one time.

SVGA (super VGA)   A computer screen standard that is usually defined as 1,024 pixels across by 768 pixels down.

tape drive   The device that reads and writes data and programs on magnetic tape.

TCP   See transmission control protocol.

TCP/IP   The two main protocols, or rules, that describe how transmissions should be handled on the Internet. See transmission control protocol; internet protocol.

telecommunications   The merger of telephone communications and computers. Refers to communication among computers using phone lines.

telecommuting   Using telecommunications and a computer at home as a substitute for working in an office outside the home.

teleconferencing   A combination of telecommunications and computer systems for holding conferences by linking geographically separated people.

telnet   Software that connects a local computer to a remote host computer. The local computer then acts as a terminal to the host. Used over the Internet.

terminal   A keyboard and screen, from which a user does work, that is connected to a minicomputer, mainframe, or supercomputer.

timesharing   A system that enables multiple users to be linked simultaneously to one computer such as a mainframe or minicomputer. Each user has his or her own terminal but shares the CPU in the mainframe or minicomputer. This system enables the CPU to switch its attention from one terminal to another to perform a small part of each user's task in a short, specified period of time.

top-level domain   The last part of the Internet address (URL) representing the type of entity, such as .COM, .EDU, or .ORG.

track   One of many concentric circles on the surface of a floppy or hard disk on which data is placed. Tracks are laid out when a disk is formatted.

trackball   An input device with the same function as a mouse, but instead of moving it on a flat surface, the user rolls a small ball that is exposed on top. Often found on or next to portable computer keyboards.

transmission control protocol (TCP)   A communications standard that handles larger blocks of data than the IP standard by breaking the large blocks into pieces. Each piece is assigned a number so the transmission can be accurately reassembled on the receiving end.

true color graphics   A photo-quality, bitmapped graphics standard that can display up to 16 million colors. Requires 24 bits of information for each pixel on the screen.

uniform-resource locator (URL)   The unique address of an Internet resource.

unshielded twisted-pair wire   A cable similar to telephone wire that is used to connect computers in a network.

upload   The act of sending a file from a node on a network to the central server.

URL   *See* uniform resource locator.

Usenet   A computer network separate from the Internet but to which most Internet users have access. Similar to a giant bulletin board, it is used for exchanging articles of common interest.

user   A person who uses a computer.

vector graphics   Produced by drawing software. All drawn objects are stored as mathematical formulas that describe their shape and color. When a vector graphic picture is loaded, the drawing software performs calculations to determine which pixels need to be activated to recreate all objects. Not as realistic as bitmapped graphic pictures, but much easier to manipulate.

VGA   Stands for video graphics array, a computer screen standard that can display 640 pixels across by 480 pixels down.

videoconferencing   Computer conferencing combined with full-motion video cameras.

WAN   *See* wide area network.

web   *See* World Wide Web.

web site   A domain's location as represented on the World Wide Web.

what-if analysis   The process of changing spreadsheet values and observing the resulting effect of the automatic recalculations.

wide area network (WAN)   A network that connects computers across a city, a state, or even the world. Consists of computers of almost any size and often includes LANs.

window   A rectangular area in the desktop of a graphical user interface. Contains a program or document.

Windows 3.1   A popular operating environment that greatly extended the capabilities of DOS. Programs and data are contained in windows. Many operations, such as starting a program, are performed by selecting icons or by choosing commands from menus.

Windows 95   Version of Windows released in August 1995 that was a complete graphical operating system and did not require DOS.

Windows 98   Version of Windows released in 1998 that is a complete graphical operating system. It significantly integrates the Internet.

Windows NT   The version of Microsoft Windows specifically designed as a network operating system (NOS) for corporate environments.

wireless   Transmitting data over networks without the use of physical connections.

word processing software   The most widely used microcomputer application software. Allows a user to create, edit, format, and print text.

workstation   In a network, the computer at which a user works. Also called a client computer. In the engineering and architectural fields, refers to a powerful, single-user, large-screen computer used for designing.

World Wide Web (WWW)   A subset of the Internet that uses text, images, sound, and video to represent data. Most sites use hyperlinks to provide easy connection to related information.

WWW   *See* World Wide Web.

Index

Photo Credits

Figure 1 Courtesy of Cray Research
2 Courtesy of IBM
3 Courtesy of Toshiba
6 Courtesy of MicroSoft Corporation
7 © Peter Steiner
8 Courtesy of Kensington
9 Courtesy of Cirque Corporation
10 Photos courtesy of Pilot Corporation
11 (a) Courtesy of Hewlett-Packard Company
    (b) Courtesy of Visioneer Communications, Inc.
    (c) Courtesy of Logitech, Inc.
12 Courtesy of Advanced Micro Devices, Inc.
13 Courtesy of Toshiba
14 (a) Courtesy of NEC Technologies
    (b) Courtesy of IBM
    (c) Courtesy of IBM
15 Courtesy of Hewlett-Packard Company
17 Courtesy of Hewlett-Packard Company
19 Courtesy of Quantum Corporation
21 Courtesy of Seagate Technology Corporation
24 (a) Courtesy of 3M
    (b) Courtesy of Inmac
    (c) Courtesy of BASF
25 Courtesy of Iomega Corporation
29 (a) © Fredrik D. Bodin
    (b) © Courtesy of Inmac
32 Courtesy of Inmac
33 Courtesy of IBM
44 Courtesy of Corel
45 Courtesy of Autodesk, Inc.
46 © Erfert Fenton
47 Courtesy of Unisys
48 Reprinted from Popular Electronics, January 1975. © Ziff-Davis Publishing Co.
49 Courtesy of John Greenleigh/Apple Computer, Inc.
50 Courtesy of Sun Microsystems, Inc.
53 Courtesy of Intel
54 Courtesy of IBM
56 Courtesy of Apple Computer
59 Courtesy of Connectix
60 Cardiff University/Australian Information Service
62 Courtesy of Instructional Design Consultants